DOSTOEVSKY AS A TRANSLATOR OF BALZAC

Studies in Comparative Literature and Intellectual History

Series Editor
Galin Tihanov (Queen Mary, University of London)

DOSTOEVSKY AS A TRANSLATOR OF BALZAC

Julia Titus

BOSTON
2022

This book is published with the assistance of the Frederick W. Hilles Publication Fund at Yale University

Library of Congress Cataloging-in-Publication Data

Names: Titus, Julia, author.
Title: Dostoevsky as a translator of Balzac / Julia Titus.
Description: Boston : Academic Studies Press, 2022. | Series: Studies in comparative literature and intellectual history | Includes bibliographical references.
Identifiers: LCCN 2021053604 (print) | LCCN 2021053605 (ebook) | ISBN 9781644697795 (hardback) | ISBN 9781644697801 (adobe pdf) | ISBN 9781644697818 (epub)
Subjects: LCSH: Dostoyevsky, Fyodor, 1821-1881--Literary style. | Balzac, Honoré de, 1799-1850 Eugénie Grandet. | Balzac, Honoré de, 1799-1850--Translations into Russian--History and criticism. | LCGFT: Literary criticism.
Classification: LCC PG3328.Z7 L2683 2022 (print) | LCC PG3328.Z7 (ebook) | DDC 891.73/3--dc23/eng/20211201
LC record available at https://lccn.loc.gov/2021053604
LC ebook record available at https://lccn.loc.gov/2021053605

ISBN 9781644697795 (hardback)
ISBN 9781644697801 (adobe pdf)
ISBN 9781644697818 (epub)

Book design by Lapiz Digital Services
Cover design by Ivan Grave

Academic Studies Press
1577 Beacon Street
Brookline, MA 02446, USA
press@academicstudiespress.com
www.academicstudiespress.com

Contents

Acknowledgements

Many people have contributed to the preparation of this book at various stages. The project was conceived at the Comparative Literature department at the Graduate Center of the City University of New York. I am deeply grateful to the faculty members there with whom I worked especially closely – André Aciman, Elizabeth Beaujour and Giancarlo Lombardi, who were always very generous with their time and advice, read multiple drafts of my work early on and offered valuable comments and feedback.

I am very thankful to the amazing editorial staff at Academic Studies Press. I would like to thank Igor Nemirovsky for his unwavering support, guidance and encouragement throughout the publishing process, and my series editor Galin Tihanov whose insightful suggestions have helped me in my work. I also owe a debt of gratitude to Brian Baer whose thorough and constructive critique played an important role in shaping the final version of the book.

I would like to express my deep appreciation to my editor Ekaterina Yanduganova, who followed the publication process closely from the beginning, and my copy editors Sasha Shapiro and Steward Allen for their great diligence and care in the editing process. I would like to thank Kira Nemirovsky and Ilya Nikolaev for their expert assistance with the cover design and production.

I extend special thanks to Inessa Laskova and the members of Yale Frederick W. Hilles Publication Fund committee chaired by Irene Peirano Garrison for their assistance with the publication of this book. I am also grateful to all my colleagues and friends at the Slavic department at Yale for fostering a nurturing and stimulating atmosphere of intellectual exchange and inquiry, and especially to John MacKay, who as a chairman of the department strongly supported my work and gave me invaluable advice.

Finally, I would like to thank my family - my parents who always encouraged my studies, and my husband Don Titus and my daughters Helena and Marianna, whose love and support have been a source of inspiration to me throughout the years that it took to complete the book.

Introduction

Transplanting any foreign masterpiece into a different language and cultural context presents many challenges for the translator and for the reader. Both have to negotiate meaning; among the many issues that a translator has to solve, foremost is the choice of whether to "transplant" the text, making it belong to the "new" culture and thus lose its foreignness, or on the contrary, to keep the the translation as close to the source text as as possible by preserving its original linguistic and syntactic structure, and thus inevitably making it "foreign" to the reader in the target language. There are also many factors in the new literature and culture that impact both the translator's work and the readers' perception, such as linguistic proximity of the source to the target language, the cultural similarity, historical context, shared cognitive concepts, ethical values, and beliefs.[1] At the same time, one of the most important factors that influences the quality and the subsequent fate of the translated work is the translator's individual literary style and talent.

Throughout the history of Russian literature, many great authors also undertook translating projects and left a remarkable legacy of literary translations in poetry and prose. Most famous among these projects are Vasily Zhukovsky's *Ludmila* (1808) and *Svetlana* (1813), free translations of ballads by Gottfried August Burger that subsequently became far more known than their German originals, and Mikhail Lermontov's free translations of Heine and Goethe. Twentieth-century examples include the celebrated translations of Shakespeare by Boris Pasternak and Vladimir Nabokov's numerous body of works as a translator (his Russian translation of *Alice in Wonderland* and his English translation of *Eugene Onegin* are just some of the more known examples), as well as his experience of self-translation in

---

1   For more on the factors influencing text translatability see Emily Apter, *The Translation Zone* (Princeton, NJ: Princeton UP, 2006).

the three versions of his autobiography. Young Dostoevsky's translation of *Eugénie Grandet* is also part of this tradition.

The translation legacy of these great authors demonstrates convincingly that a good literary translator always has a dynamic and creative relationship with the original text, and a certain degree of translator's freedom is necessary. It is permissible to deviate from the letter of the original in order to bring out its spirit. By working actively with the text, the translator brings the reader closer to an understanding and appreciation of the original work: "we are led . . . back to the source text: the circle within which the approximation of the foreign and the familiar, the known and the unknown constantly move, is finally complete."[2]

At the same time, the translators cannot disregard the existing reading tradition and cultural expectation of their compatriots, so that the newly translated work continues in some ways the existing literary canon and adds to the already established literary legacy of a specific country. In his essay "Russkaia literatura na frantsuzskom iazyke" Yuri Lotman noted that after reforms of Peter the Great, Russian culture was "developing under the sign of Europeanization," and since the eighteenth century, French language and culture became for Russians the ideal symbol of Europe.[3] This was certainly true for young Dostoevsky, who was an avid reader of many French authors, and especially Honoré de Balzac, whose books he admired and continued to read throughout his life. Our analysis of Dostoevsky's translation will demonstrate that the young Dostoevsky was influenced, on the one hand, by French ideas, and on the other hand, by the Russian Orthodox values and beliefs that were crucial for his own intellectual development, and this was reflected in the way he chose to approach *Eugénie Grandet* while translating it for Russian readers. Thus, Dostoevsky's free translation can be seen as an amalgam of French ideas and cultural notions transplanted into Russian soil and viewed through the lense of Dostoevsky's Christian Orthodox philosophy and Russian cultural tradition.

In his multi-volume biography of Dostoevsky, Joseph Frank wrote: "No predecessor in the European novel was more important for Dostoevsky than Balzac, and such works as *Eugénie Grandet* and *Le Père Goriot* were

---

2   Lawrence Venuti, *The Translation Studies Reader* (London: Routledge, 2000), 66.

3   "Until the middle of the nineteenth century, the French language was the bridge for the movement of ideas and cultural values from Europe into Russia." Iurii Lotman, *Izbrannye stat'i*, vol. 2 (Tallinn, Estonia: Aleksandra, 1992), 368.

to serve as trail-blazers clearing the path for his own productions."[4] In August of 1838, having read almost all of Balzac's works, Dostoevsky wrote to his brother Mikhail: "Бальзак велик! Его характеры—произведения ума вселенной. Не дух времени, но целые тысячелетия приготовили борением своим такую развязку в душе человека"[5] (Balzac is great! His characters are the creation of the mind of the universe. Not just the spirit of the time but whole millennia prepared by their struggle this outcome of the human soul). In the 1840s, Dostoevsky asked his friend and fellow writer Dmitry Grigorovich to send him some books by Balzac, "I would like to reread *César Birotteau* and *Mercadet*." Many years after completing the translation, in 1880, Dostoevsky answered the question of his young friend, the writer and memoirist Vera Mikulich, "Ну, а кого вы ставите выше, Бальзака или себя?" (Whom do you consider higher, Balzac or yourself?), with "Каждый из нас дорог только в той мере, в которой он принес в литературу что-нибудь свое, что-нибудь оригинальное. В этом все. А сравнивать нас я не могу. Думаю, что у каждого есть свои заслуги"[6] (Each of us is valuable only to the degree that he brought into literature something uniquely his own, something original. That is all. I cannot compare us. I believe that we each have our own merit). In her memoir, Mikulich also remembers that Dostoevsky recommended that she read *Le Père Goriot* shortly before he died. Balzac remained a very strong influence for Dostoevsky throughout his life.

Balzac's work was quite popular in Russia and his arrival in Russia was widely anticipated. Pushkin's sister Maria wrote to her husband already in 1836: "à propos, nous attendons Balzac; on prétend qu'il est déjà a Kiev"[7] (By the way, we are expecting Balzac; they say he is already in Kiev). In 1838, a fictitious article "Balzac dans la province de Kherson" appeared in a major Saint Petersburg literary journal *Sovremennik* (The contemporary) describing Balzac's visit to Kherson in Ukraine, even though he never visited there. The article claimed that Balzac had a huge success with the local ladies who could name all his works in chronological order, knew all the characters in *La Comédie humaine*, and could even recite the best pages

---

4   Joseph Frank, *The Seeds of Revolt: 1821–1849* (Princeton, NJ: Princeton UP, 1979), 106.
5   Leonid Grossman, *Dostoevskii. Put'. Poetika. Tvorchestvo* (Moscow, Russia: Sovremennye problemy, 1928), 234.
6   Vera Mikulich, *Vstrechi c pisateliami* (Leningrad: Izdatel'stvo pisatelei, 1929), 155.
7   Leonid Grossman, *Balzac en Russie* (Paris, France: Presse française et étrangère, 1946), 35.

by heart: "Les dames de la province de Kherson sont folles de Balzac. Vous n'avez qu'à prononcer le nom du nouvelist français pour voir à quelle point les dames de l'aristocratie se passionnent pour lui"[8] (The ladies of Kherson are crazy about Balzac. You only have to mention the name of French novelist to see how passionately the ladies of the aristocracy feel about him). This episode illustrates to what degree the name of Balzac was already known and popular among the Russian audience not just in the capital, but in the regions as well.

The leading Russian literary magazines were interested in providing Russian translations of Balzac's novels for their audience. At the same time, the fairly large percent of the educated reading public of Russia who spoke French fluently had the opportunity to acquaint themselves with Balzac's novels almost as soon as they appeared in France, thanks to the French-language literary magazine that was published in Russia, *Revue étrangere de littérature, des sciences et des arts*. Balzac's novels were highly regarded by many Russian authors, including Ivan Turgenev, Ivan Goncharov, and later Maxim Gorky. Leo Tolstoy expressed great admiration for *La Comédie humaine*, and Ivan Goncharov wrote that he decided to become a writer after reading and rereading *La Peau de Chagrin* and *Eugénie Grandet*. Balzac's enormous, enduring popularity in Russia is evoked much later in Chekhov's *Three Sisters*, where Chebutykin reads in the old newspaper that "Balzac was married in Berdichev."

Balzac had plans to visit Russia for quite some time because of his long romantic attachment to Evelyne Hanska, who permanently resided in her great Ukrainian estate Wierzchownia but was a frequent visitor to Saint Petersburg. In 1842, Balzac received news that Madame Hanska's husband had died, and he decided to travel to Saint Petersburg so that he could obtain permission to marry her and possibly move to Russia himself. In addition, Balzac's own interests in Saint Petersburg, which he viewed as the cultural and political center of northern Europe, and his multiple projects regarding diplomacy and commerce, all influenced his desire to travel to Russia. As Leonid Grossman in his study *Balzac en Russie* explains about Balzac's desire to visit Russia: "Il [Balzac] rêvait de créer en Russie une litérature, une théâtre et une presse du type européen. Il se rendait compte qu'il était populaire dans les pays du Nord"[9] ("He dreamed of creating in

---

8   Ibid., 68.
9   Ibid., 28.

Russia the European-style literature, theater and press. He realized that he was popular in the northern countries.")[10]

Going to Russia, Balzac hoped to resolve his material difficulties, and to forget his disappointment with the French political regime of the period. But most importantly, he envisioned for himself an active role as a figure of political importance and cultural influence. Balzac spent ten weeks in Saint Petersburg in the fall of 1843, the same year young Dostoevsky began working on the first Russian translation of *Eugénie Grandet*. Unfortunately, while Balzac was at the center of Russian literary life, none of his commercial or political hopes materialized, and he was received coldly by Russian official circles. Later Balzac said that he received a slap in the face intended for the Marquis de Custine, for discussing Russian hostility to the French in general after the Marquis de Custine published his famous book *La Russie en 1839*, which was sharply critical of Nikolas I's Russia that he saw during his travels.

Balzac's *Eugénie Grandet* was hailed as a masterpiece even before it was translated into Russian. *Severnaya pchela* (The Northern bee), one of the most influential Russian literary magazines of that time, wrote: "От всей души сознаёмся, что видим в нем одного из лучших романистов нашего века. *Eugénie Grandet*, *Histoire des Treize* и множество других романов доставили автору неувядаемый венок"[11] (We admit wholeheartedly that we see in him one of the best novelists of our century. *Eugénie Grandet*, *Histoire des Treize* and many other novels brought to the author eternal laurels). Senkovsky, the editor of another influential literary magazine, *Biblioteka dlya chteniya* (Library for reading), called *Eugénie Grandet* Balzac's best novel.

The popularity of Balzac in Russia, and the general excitement surrounding that particular novel, explained why young Dostoevsky received a higher than usual honorarium for his work as its translator. His translation of *Evgenia Grande* was published in the summer of 1844 in two volumes of the literary magazine *Repertuar i panteon*, volumes 6 and 7, without the name of a translator but with the following introductory note from the editor: "Это один из первых, и бесспорно, из лучших романов плодовитого Бальзака, который в последнее время заметно исписался. Сколько нам известно, роман этот в русском переводе

---

10 Translation mine.
11 Leonid Grossman, *Dostoevskii* (Moscow: Molodaia gvardiia, 1965), 235.

напечатан не был, а поэтому мы надеемся угодить многим из наших читателей, поместив его в 'Репертуар и Пантеон'" (This is one of the first and undoubtedly the best novels of prolific Balzac, who as of late has noticeably written himself out. As far as we know, this novel has not been translated into Russian, and therefore we hope to please many of our readers by publishing it in *Repertuar i panteon*).[12] By that time, there existed three book editions of the novel in French (1834, 1839, and 1843). In the first edition, the text was divided into chapters, each of which had a separate title: 1. "Physiognomies bourgeoises," 2. "Le Cousin de Paris," 3. "Amours de Province," 4. "Promesses d'avare, serments d'amour," 5. "Chagrins de famille," 6. "Aussi va le monde," and 7. "Conclusion." In the revised 1839 edition, Balzac eliminated the chapter divisions, supposedly for conserving space. In subsequent editions, the division was not restored, and the last chapter got considerably shorter. Since Dostoevsky was working with the first edition of 1834, he kept the initial chapter division. There is one other difference between the first edition and the subsequent versions of *Eugénie Grandet*: at the end of the novel, there is discussion of a Greek statue, which is completely omitted starting from the edition of 1839. It is kept but shortened in Dostoevsky's translation. Finally, in the 1843 edition, when *Eugénie Grandet* was published among the other novels of *La Comédie humaine*, it was made part of a series called *Scènes de la vie de province*. No indication of that is found in the Russian translation.

The translation of *Eugénie Grandet* in 1844 was Dostoevsky's first published work. While living in Saint Petersburg after graduation from the Military Engineering Academy, young Dostoevsky initially took up translating as a supplemental source of income in addition to his modest salary as an engineer. He and his brother Mikhail made ambitious plans to translate and publish works of popular French and German authors. They selected the novels based on their personal preference and the potential interest for Russian readers. It was thought that Mikhail will do translations from German, and Dostoevsky would do French. One of the first novels that Dostoevsky proposed to Mikhail for translation and publication in Russia through their joint translation enterprise was Eugene Sue's novel *Mathilde*. Eugene Sue was widely read in Russia, and young Dostoevsky was an avid reader of Sue's novels. Sue's technique of *roman-feuilleton* with a cliffhanger ending of the episode at the most climactic moments, as well

---

12 Translation mine.

as his eloquent descriptions of cities and portrayals of extreme poverty and richness, was incorporated by Dostoevsky in his own writing. Echoes of the *Mathilde*'s plot about the friendship between a poor girl and her rich friend is echoed in *Netochka Nezvanova* (1849), Dostoevsky's first unfinished novel about an orphan who is taken in by a rich relative. Dostoevsky began translating Sue's novel but soon abandoned the project because of lack of funds.

In 1844, Dostoevsky began to work on a translation of George Sand's novel *La Dernière Aldini*, a complicated love story between an aristocrat and a fisherman set in Venice during the time of Italy's unification. The novels of George Sand were beloved by Russian readers, and Dostoevsky hoped for the translation's quick commercial success. Unfortunately, once he finished his translation, he discovered to his great disappointment that this novel had already been translated into Russian, so it was not possible to publish his translation. Dostoevsky also had the idea of translating the complete works of Schiller and publishing them in Russia. Mikhail would be the translator and he the publisher. Mikhail translated *The Robbers* and *Don Carlos* and published the dramas in the Russian journals, but the plan for publication of the complete works of Schiller never came to fruition. Thus, *Evgenia Grande* was Dostoevsky's only successful venture in his career as a translator.

However, the experience of translating literary texts remained an important milestone for Dostoevsky. Brian Baer mentions that Dostoevsky even made a theme of literary translation appear in his novels.[13] For example, thirty years later, Verkhovensky, one of Dostoevsky's characters in *The Demons* (1872), recalls the same experience of translating George Sand when he was young. Similarly, in *Crime and Punishment* (1866) Razumikhin knows three European languages and works as a freelance translator. He even offers Raskolnikov a job translating from German, which Raskolnikov declines. When Razumikhin describes his work on translations to Raskolnikov, he says that he does not have sufficient knowledge of German and frequently has to make things up as he goes along, but he "takes the only comfort in thinking that it improves the text"[14] ("только

---

13 Brian Baer, *Translation and the Making of the Modern Russian Literature* (New York: Bloomsbury Academic, 2015), 91–92.
14 Translation mine.

тем и утешаюсь, что от этого еще лучше выходит").[15] Razumikhin's speech is clearly intended as a parody on what a good translation should be because immediately after that he proceeds to describe the unscrupulous publisher Kheruvimov who makes money by quickly responding to what the general Russian readers are currently interested in. For example, the German treatise that Razumikhin offers Raskolnikov discusses "whether a woman can be considered a human being"[16] and relates to "women's rights question"; similarly, future plans of translation from Kheruvimov involve offering the Russian public a pastiche of "most boring gossips" from *Confessions* by Rousseau. Translation in *Crime and Punishment* is clearly presented as a parody of the original, and that is why, perhaps, Raskolnikov turns it down, saying "I don't need translation."

Dostoevsky started to work on the translation of *Eugénie Grandet* at the end of 1843, inspired by Balzac's recent visit to Saint Petersburg earlier that year. He completed the translation very quickly and wrote enthusiastically to his brother Mikhail in the beginning of 1844: "Нужно тебе знать, что на праздниках я перевел 'Евгению Grandet' Бальзака (чудо! чудо!) перевод бесподобный" (You should know that over the holidays I translated *Evgenia Grandet* [*sic*] by Balzac [a marvel! a marvel!] the translation is superb).[17]

In order to better understand the significance of Dostoevsky's translation, it may be helpful to look briefly at the further history and evolution of the Russian translations of *Eugénie Grandet* (predominantly known in Russia as *Evgenia Grande*). Currently there are three known versions of *Eugénie Grandet* in Russian: Fyodor Dostoevsky's translation was published in 1844, Isaya Mandelshtam's, in 1927, and Yuri Verkhovsky's, in 1935. The latter is still considered the canonical version.[18] Dostoevsky's first translation reflects the nineteenth-century notion of the Romantic period where the ideal translation aimed at bringing a foreign text to the reader, "domesticating" it; thus, the translator was seen also as a commentator and co-creator. If one looks at Alexander Pushkin's or Mikhail Lermontov's translations of French and German poets, one sees that their free translations are

---

15 Fedor Dostoevskii, *Sobranie sochinenii v 15 tomakh* (Leningrad, Russia: Nauka, 1989–1996), vol. 5, 49.

16 Ibid.

17 Translation mine.

18 For more see Aleksandra Leshnevskaia, "Tri 'Grande,'" *Inostrannaia literatura* 4 (2008), http://magazines.russ.ru/inostran/2008/4/le5.html.

essentially new and beautiful poems that stand alongside the original and can be read independently. Dostoevsky approached Balzac's masterpiece with a similar creative freedom.

When young Dostoevsky began his work on the translation, his aim was to make Balzac's original text, which was densely populated with uniquely French details, completely understandable for Russian readers unfamiliar with French realia. In terms of today's translation theory, Dostoevsky was using the approach that Lawrence Venuti defined as "bringing the text to the reader."[19] In keeping with this theoretical premise, Dostoevsky even Russified the first name of Balzac's protagonist, changing it from Eugénie to the Russian Evgenia. Working with the aim to make the text accessible to the Russian general public, Dostoevsky eliminated some obscure names of textiles, some descriptions of wine-making terms and barrel-making techniques, as well as other words and concepts that were difficult to understand for Russian readers without extensive commentary and explanatory notes (such as *noblesse de cloche*—lit. "nobility of the bell," or municipal nobility, conferred to the mayor and other municipal officials of certain historically important French towns; *poinçon de vin*—a wine glass holding 250 milliliters; *halleboteur*—"grape-gleaner"; *une truisse*—a regional word meaning "tree hedge," and so forth). The main characters also received Russian names, and began to use diminutive suffixes, again part of the attempt to make the translation read like a Russian novel. For example, in Dostoevsky's translation, Old Grandet calls his daughter жизнёночек мой (lit. "my little life"), while in Balzac's text Grandet calls her *ma fifille*. The Russian word is unusual and is taken from Dostoevsky's father's letters to his wife, while the French is fully standard meaning "my little girl." Notwithstanding his idiosyncratic choices, Dostoevsky's conscious strategy of substituting French idioms by Russian ones made the text more understandable for the Russian reader.

The result of his creative work was a free translation that many critics faulted as being too free and taking too many liberties with the original—hence not a true translation but a retelling of the story. After the initial publication in the Saint Petersburg literary journal *Repertuar i panteon* in 1844, Dostoevsky's translation was forgotten until 2014, when a new edition of his translation appeared in Saint Petersburg.

---

19 Venuti, *The Translation Studies Reader*, 49.

In the late 1920s in Russia, the opposite view of maximally precise translation being the best became dominant, and a new movement of *bukvalizm* (literalness), taking its name from the Russian word for letter, *bukva*, was born. Following one of its main theorists, translator Evgeny Lann, the new movement prized the literal precision of translation at the expense of its readability and advocated keeping the original "foreign " terms. Dostoevsky's translation of Balzac was widely rebuked, and a new translation of the novel by Isaya Mandelshtam was published in 1927.[20] Following the new trend, even the name of the titular character was approximated to French pronunciation and transcribed in Cyrillic as Ezheni Grande (Эжени Гранде). While Dostoevsky in his translation of the novel strove to Russify the text by giving many Russian diminutive suffixes and realia, Isaya Mandelshtam, under the influence of *bukvalizm*, deliberately included in his translation a lot of French borrowings, thus choosing to highlight the French origin of the novel.

Soon after that, the *bukvalist* movement was supplanted by the new school of translation that aimed to harmoniously connect the two opposing views: readability on the one hand, and on the other, respect for the foreign realia present in the original. The last Russian translation of *Eugénie Grandet* by Yuri Verkhovsky in 1935 reflects this approach. This last translation remains canonical for the Russian readers and has been reprinted numerous times.

One should note that many textual changes that occurred to the Russian versions of *Eugénie Grandet* are not the only such case of a foreign classical novel with several Russian translations. Marina Kostomarova in her article "Charles Dickens in Nineteenth-Century Russia" similarly highlights significant transformations of *The Pickwick Papers* throughout different Russian versions.[21] In her study of Dickens's reception in Russia, Kostomarova demonstrates that this dynamic process of shaping and reshaping the source text through translation also forms the literary reputation of the author in the target culture. At the same time, the historical and cultural context in which the translation first appeared is also very influential, as we have seen with the three Russian versions of *Eugénie Grandet*.

---

20 For more about this period, see Andrei Azov, *Poverzhennye bykvalisty* (Moscow, Russia: Izdatel'skii dom Vysshei Shkoly Ekonomiki, 2013).
21 Brian Baer and Susanna Witt, eds., *Translation in Russian Contexts* (New York and London: Routledge, 2018), 110–125.

Susan Bassnett in her 1998 work *Constructing Cultures: Essays on Literary Translation*, written with André Lefevere, argues for translator-centered texts and discusses the shift of emphasis from original to translation and the degree of the visibility of the translator in the text. Similarly, Emily Apter in *Translation Zone* points out the inherent tension between textual and cultural translation, and notes that texts that are more culturally loaded present more challenges to translators, making the role of the translator paramount in negotiating meaning.

Dostoevsky's translation clearly belongs to translator-centered texts. If one looks closely at his work, one can immediately see that Dostoevsky consciously changed the original in many ways to make it maximally accessible to the Russian readers. This study analyzes specific textual changes and conscious departures from the original that Dostoevsky made to accomplish his task, as well as investigates the reasons behind his choices and the difference that they make in the experience of reading Balzac's novel in Russian versus the original French.

While several studies exist on the translation of Dostoevsky's novels into different languages, there is almost nothing written about his work as a translator. He first took up translating as a source of income, but for his projects he only chose those authors for whom he felt a deep admiration and affinity, such as Honoré de Balzac and George Sand. Young Dostoevsky's choice is not surprising, since he named Balzac as one of his favorite authors while he was still in high school. Both Balzac and George Sand were deeply interested in the psychological and emotional development of their characters, as well as the effects of society and wealth on the individual, social issues, and love as a force that transcends the obstacles of convention and social class. These major themes later became very important for Dostoevsky's own writings.

Consequently, this book also analyzes Dostoevsky's first literary publication as a crucible for his own literary style. Judith Woodsworth points out that "writers have always regarded translation as an exercise, as a prelude to and preparation for original work, in short, as *pre-text*. Alternatively, they have seen it as *pretext* for something else, as a way of paying tribute to an admired foreign writer, as an infusion of elements of foreign culture into their own culture, or as a mechanism for strengthening personal or collective identity."[22] In my view, it is valuable to study Dostoevsky's translation from this perspective, focusing specifically on how it accomplishes both of the objectives identified by Woodsworth—it functions as a *pretext* for Dostoevsky's subsequent development as a writer, and at the same time it weaves Balzac's themes into Russian cultural context, giving them new dimensions.

Dostoevsky's work on Balzac's original text had a profound impact on his own writing. This comparative study aims to trace the connections between Balzac's techniques of creating his characters and the fictional spaces of his novels and the ways in which they are echoed in Dostoevsky's later novels, sometimes explicitly referencing Balzac's style and in other instances subconsciously. We can see the beginnings of Dostoevsky's own literary style and poetics in the ways that he approached the translation of Balzac.

In this first publication of young Dostoevsky, one can already observe some antecedents of his future poetics. For example, Dostoevsky approached Balzac's long descriptions with great freedom, and he frequently changed the syntactic structure of the sentences by eliminating or adding words or by substituting the epithets in Balzac's original with several Russian adjectives. At the same time, he amplified the emotional tension in the novel and focused his attention fully on the theme of self-sacrifice, love, and faith. In his translation, one can see the brilliant treatment of dialogue and a very active narrative voice. These would later become distinguishing stylistic features of Dostoevsky's own novels.

Balzac's view of the role of the writer is also relevant to Dostoevsky's own beliefs. In his foreword to *La Comédie humaine*, Balzac describes the role of the author as a "secretary" who is transcribing the history of society: "La société française allait être l'historien, je ne devais être que le secrétaire" (The French society was going to be the historian; I was supposed to be nothing but a secretry).[23] This point resembles Dostoevsky's own position when he referred to the writer as a "stenographer" ("The Meek One"). The author draws the readers' attention to his creative method in the Introduction to "The Meek One": "Вот это предположение о записавшем всё стенографе (после которого я обделал бы записанное) и есть то, что я называю в

---

22 Judith Woodsworth, *Telling the Story of Translation: Writers who Translate* (London, UK: Bloomsbury Academic, 2017), 5–6.

23 Honoré de Balzac, "L'Avant-propos de 'La Comédie humaine,'" in his *Oeuvres completes* (Paris, France: Les Bibliophiles de l'origine, 1965), 14.

этом рассказе фантастическим" (This assumption about a stenographer, whose record I then would have polished, is what I call in this story fantastic). Dostoevsky published "The Meek One" in his *Diary of a Writer*, where he also recorded his own observations of Saint Petersburg life and chronicles from daily newspapers that provided factual material for his stories and polemical essays. This creative method of drawing ideas for his stories and novels from the current events in Saint Petersburg life also connects Dostoevsky and Balzac, who, in Zweig's words, was an "observer of the pageant of life"[24] and used his exceptional power of observation to recreate the fictional world of *La Comédie humaine.*

Young Dostoevsky's intensive work on Balzac's novel provided some of the paradigms through which he would affirm his own talent as a writer later. One can look at the main characters in *Evgenia Grande* as the prototypes of Dostoevsky's later novels, specifically the self-sacrificing and loving Evgenia and her despotic father, driven by his singular mania of avarice to unnatural cruelty towards his daughter. The motif of a "quiet" family drama where all family relationships are broken would reappear repeatedly in Dostoevsky's novels. Balzac's intense interest in the physical environment of his characters and its direct connection to their inner world is another device that later Dostoevsky would also employ in his works.

An important element that develops in Dostoevsky's close interaction with Balzac's text and then resurfaces in his own works is approaching characters as archetypes. It is known that Balzac worked on several editions of his novel with an aim to make Grandet less of a one-dimensional miser and villain and more of a complex, multifaceted character. When Balzac refers to Old Grandet, he calls him *monsieur Grandet, bonhomme, maître de la maison, l'oncle, le vigneron, le tonnelier* (Mr. Grandet, good man, master of the house, uncle, winemaker, barrel maker) to avoid focusing only on his avarice and not to emulate too closely archetypical misers such as Molière's Harpagon. Dostoevsky, on the contrary, highlights Grandet's monomania and makes obsession with money his salient characteristic. Instead of Balzac's many references, Dostoevsky only uses one epithet, *скряга* (miser), multiple times throughout the novel. The character of Eugénie is treated in a similar archetypal manner. Dostoevsky omits all the allusions to the sensual pleasures of love that Eugénie dreams about and makes his character very chaste, pure, and virtuous. In her devotion, chastity, and sacrifice, she

---

24 Stefan Zweig, *Balzac* (New York: Viking, 1946), 176.

resembles the idealized self-sacrificing and suffering women of Dostoevsky's own novels (Alyosha's mother in *Brothers Karamazov*, the nameless central character in *The Meek One*, Sonya in *Crime and Punishment*)

Another common point in terms of character creation for Balzac and Dostoevsky is their shared interest in *théorie du milieu*—an aesthetic principle that posits a strong connection between characters and their environment. Very specific detailed descriptions of the setting before the characters appear and the plot unfolds became Balzac's signature device. In *Eugénie Grandet* this artistic device is employed in the opening of the novel, where a detailed description of Saumur is presented on several pages. The author then dwells on the particular melancholic look of its houses before finally focusing on the house of the main character: ". . . vous apercevez un renforcement aussi sombre, au centre duquel est cachée la porte de la maison à monsieur Grandet. Il est impossible de comprendre la valeur de cette expression provinciale sans donner la biographie de monsieur Grandet"[25] (you will see a somewhat dark recess, in the center of which is hidden the door of the house of Monsier Grandet. It is impossible to understand the force of this provincial expression without giving the biography of Monsier Grandet).[26] Dostoevsky employed the same technique in his novels and stories, as evidenced by his meticulous descriptions of Saint Petersburg streets and buildings (see *Poor Folk*, The Double, and *White Nights*, the novels written in 1845–1848, shortly after the publication of his translation, or *Crime and Punishment*). His descriptions do not merely create for the reader an impression of the physical setting of the plot, but make the city itself one of the characters in the story. Dostoevsky's depictions of the characters' houses and atmosphere inside are directly connected to their inner world.

The theme of money is another element that is very important for Balzac, just as it is for Dostoevsky's own works. In Dostoevsky's major novels, attitude to money becomes the primary vehicle for character exploration and functions as the litmus test for a character's integrity, morality, and humanity. Motives of money and avarice allow Dostoevsky to create such brilliant plot nodes as the murder in *The Brothers Karamazov* or the money-burning scene with Nastasya Filippovna in *The Idiot*, and such memorable characters as Fyodor Karamazov, driven by money and lust,

---

25 Honoré de Balzac, *Eugénie Grandet* (Paris, France: Mme. Charles-Béchet, 1834), 6.
26 Translation mine.

or the proud pawnbroker in *The Meek One* for whom money becomes the primary means of relating to others. For Dostoevsky as a writer, avarice is the top human vice, and it is only natural that he adopts Balzac's mysterious and evil figure of a pawnbroker who inspires hatred and fear, using this character as a symbol of the hidden power of money.

The theme of money is frequently linked to gambling, chance, and fate. Like the characters of Balzac, Dostoevsky's characters try their luck at cards, and much later, in 1866, Dostoevsky writes a whole novel, *The Gambler*, set in a fictional *Rulettenburg* where money, love, chance, and fate are decided at the roulette table.

Like Balzac, throughout his own novels Dostoevsky seeks to portray the human soul at the moments of greatest emotional turmoil. Dostoevsky's incessant focus on the individual's psychology juxtaposed with the keen observations of the characters' social environment can be traced to his early experience as a translator of Balzac. Thus, a close analysis of his translation is a valuable tool for literary study. The subsequent chapters will study the two texts side by side through the prism of close reading and analyze how these elements reappear in Dostoevsky's own works later on.

Chapter One

Reflections of Eugénie in Dostoevsky's Female Characters

As discussed in the introduction, Balzac was an extremely important author for Dostoevsky's own development as a writer. Young Dostoevsky's experience as a translator of *Eugénie Grandet* allowed him to immerse himself fully in Balzac's writing style, setting description, and character development, and his first close interaction with Balzac's text had a profound influence on his own later novels. This chapter focuses on tracing the influence of the main character Eugénie on Dostoevsky's images representing the ideal woman in his works.

Young Dostoevsky was attracted to Balzac's *Eugénie Grandet* because of its great emotional and psychological tension and its powerful central female character. In *Eugénie Grandet*, Balzac created a compelling portrait of a virtuous, deeply loving, and self-sacrificing woman, who in her youth briefly cherished hopes for family happiness and love, but whose aspirations and dreams were crushed, and whose unfulfilled emotional life continues for many years in quiet suffering and spiritual loneliness. The stark contrast between mature Eugénie's outward prosperity, due to the great fortune she inherited from her father, and the inner sorrow of living in complete solitude without any human affection or even hope for a more joyful future created a poignant emotional conflict and silent despair, the depth of which Dostoevsky was to recreate later in his novels.

Balzac's Eugénie and Dostoevsky's Evgenia

The analysis of the conclusion of the novel, focusing on the description of a mature Eugénie, will uncover the considerable stylistic changes, omissions, and expansions that Dostoevsky brings to the text. In the final pages of his novel, Balzac draws the portrait of a mature Eugénie, who had married M. de Bonfons but is now widowed and approaching her forties:

> Son visage est blanc, reposé, calme; sa voix douce et recueillie, ses manières simples. Elle a toutes les noblesses de la douleur, la sainteté d'une personne qui n'a pas souillé son âme au contact du monde, mais aussi la roideur de la vieille fille et les habitudes mesquines que donne l'existence étroite de la province.[1]

> (Her face is white, placid and calm. Her voice is gentle and subdued. She has the nobility of grief, the saintliness of a person whose soul has never been sullied by contact with the world, but also the stiffness of an old maid and the petty habits which are the result of a narrow provincial existence.)[2]

In his translation of this passage, as well as in many other places throughout the novel, Dostoevsky brings in several notable changes in his depiction of the mature Evgenia that would have especial significance for his own poetics as a writer later on: "Черты лица ее нежные, тихие; вокруг нее лучезарный венец благородства, мученичества; она уберегла свою душу от тлетворного влияния света; но вместе с тем в ней заметны сухость и привычки старой девы"[3] (Her facial features are tender, quiet; she has a radiant halo of nobility, of martyrdom; she has protected her soul from the corrupting influence of the world; but at the same time, one can see in her the dryness and the habits of an old maid).[4] Here Dostoevsky shortens Balzac's text and, at the same time, amplifies Eugénie's saintly character traits by adding to her portrait the radiant halo of a saint and martyr, the obligatory attribute of saints on the icons, even though that visual detail is absent in Balzac's original. Similarly, Balzac's *noblesse de la douleur*—lit. "nobility of pain"—is transformed in Dostoevsky's translation in *мученичество*—"martyrdom," strongly highlighting the religious

---

1   Fedor Dostoevskii, *Evgeniia Grande* (Saint Petersburg, Russia: Azbuka, 2014), 380.

2   Honoré de Balzac, *Père Goriot, and Eugénie Grandet* (New York: Modern Library, 1950), 495.

3   Dostoevskii, *Evgeniia Grande*, 255.

4   All translations into English from Dostoevsky's *Evgenia Grande* are mine.

attributes in his treatment of Eugénie's character and further strengthening her connection to Christian pain and suffering. These images of meek, saintly suffering and martyrdom reappears in Dostoevsky's descriptions of his virtuous and noble female characters in his novels and short stories.

Balzac's description of Eugénie as "une personne, qui n'a pas souilé son âme au contact du monde" (a person who has not sullied her soul by contact with the world) is transformed in Dostoevsky's translation so that Eugénie acquires more agency: "she has protected her soul from the corrupting influence of the world." *La roideur* is transformed into *сухость* (lit. "dryness") in Russian, whereas "rigidity" would be a more precise equivalent. Finally, Balzac's important reference to the effects that life in the province has on a person's mind ("les habitudes mesquines que donne l'existence etroite de la province") is omitted altogether, because for the majority of Dostoevsky's readers, life in the Russian province was the reality, and not many of them would have felt the disadvantages of a "narrow provincial life."

Continuing his portrait of Eugénie, Balzac employs his signature literary device: he emphasizes a strong connection between the character and her milieu or dwelling: "La maison de Saumur, maison sans soleil, sans chaleur, sans cesse ombragée, mélancolique, est l'image de sa vie"[5] (The house in Saumur, sunless and cold, always gloomy and melancholy, is symbolic of her life).[6] Dostoevsky adds to this sentence the participle *лишенный*—"deprived," which increases the coldness and the feeling of general gloom in his translation: "Сомюрский дом, лишенный света и тепла, вечно погруженный в тень и печаль,—вот прообраз ее жизни"[7] (The house in Saumur, deprived of light and warmth, eternally submerged in shadow and sadness—this is the prototype of her life). This word intensifies the metaphorical meaning of the description because in Russian it is usually applied to people, not things, and has an additional shade of meaning conveying something that was previously there but was taken away against the person's will (*узник, лишенный свободы*—"a prisoner deprived of freedom," *человек, лишенный надежды*—"a person deprived of hope," and so forth). Thus, in Dostoevsky's translation, the house of Grandet is represented as something alive that had lost its previous warmth, extending the metaphor and making an even more direct connection between Eugénie's home and her fate. The all-important

---

5   Dostoevskii, *Evgeniia Grande*, 380.

6   Balzac, *Père Goriot, and Eugénie Grandet*, 496.

7   Dostoevskii, *Evgeniia Grande*, 255.

connection between the character and his dwelling that is central to Balzac's poetics would also become very prominent in Dostoevsky's later works.[8]

Balzac then shifts the attention of his readers to Eugénie's charitable work, which he describes in considerable detail:

> Elle accumule soigneusement ses revenus, et peut-être eût-t-elle semblé parcimonieuse, si elle ne démentait la médisance par un noble emploi de sa fortune. De pieuses et charitable fondations, un hospice pour la vieillesse et des écoles chrétiennnes pour les enfants, une bibliothèque publique richement dotée témoignent chaque année contre l'avarice dont certaines personnes la soupçonnaient.[9]

> (She carefully accumulates her income, and might perhaps seem parsimonious, had such a charge not been contradicted by the noble use she made of her fortune. Pious and charitable institutions, a home for the aged, and Christian schools for children, a richly endowed public library bear witness year after year against the avarice of which some people accuse her.)[10]

In his translation, Dostoevsky shortens Balzac's specific enumeration of Eugénie's charity, and cuts out any mention of pious and charitable foundations, merely saying: "Ее могли бы прозвать скупой, если бы не было известно, на что употреблялись ее доходы. Она основала несколько школ, богаделен, публичную библиотеку. Церкви Сомюра приходят в цветущее состояние"[11] (She could have been called parsimonious if it was not generally known to everyone to what her income was employed. She founded several schools, old people's homes, a public library. The churches of Saumur are coming to a flourishing state).

Notable in Dostoevsky's translation of this excerpt is the inversion of order in which Balzac lists various charitable institutions that Eugénie founded. Instead of pious foundations and homes for the elderly, Dostoevsky's list starts with schools because, like Tolstoy, he felt that better access to public schools for peasant children was extremely important in the context of Russian life given the dismal state of education in Russian provinces. Moreover, the education of youth had to be carried

---

8   For more discussion of this topic see Chapter Two.

9   Dostoevskii, *Evgeniia Grande*, 381.

10 Balzac, *Père Goriot, and Eugénie Grandet*, 496.

11 Dostoevskii, *Evgeniia Grande*, 225.

out in accordance with Christian values to help raise the next generation of people who are highly moral and selfless. Dostoevsky's Evgenia is the embodiment of virtue and thus she is seen as an example of such highly moral individual.

Here and in other similar situations Dostoevsky chose to omit the details that seemed unclear and unnecessary to him. For example, the words "pious and charitable foundations" were eliminated for being too vague and replaced with certain specific items: schools, homes for the elderly, a library, and churches. As a writer interested mainly in the psychological development of his characters, Dostoevsky preferred to concentrate on certain focal points indicating Evgenia's emotional state. He focused his attention fully on the subsequent passages dealing with Evgenia's feelings and her stoicism in the finale of the novel.

Continuing his portrayal of Eugénie, Balzac creates an opposition between her rich emotional inner life and the external power of money and the cold calculations of reason: "Ce noble coeur, qui ne battait que pour les sentiments les plus tendres, devait donc être soumis aux calculs de l'intérêt humain. L'argent devait communiquer ses teintes froides a cette vie céleste, et lui donner de la défiance pour les sentiments"[12] (This noble heart, moved only by the tenderest feelings, was to be subjected to the calculations of human interest. Money was to pass its cool gleam to this saintly life, and teach her to distrust feelings).[13]

Dostoevsky lengthens and amplifies the ending of Balzac's last sentence in his translation:

> Но это благородное сердце, которое билось лишь для самых нежных чувств, было призвано покориться расчетам человеческой алчности. Деньги должны были сообщить свои холодные оттенки этой небесной жизни и внушить недоверие к чувствам в женщине, которая вся была чувство![14]

> (But the noble heart that was beating only for the most tender of feelings, had to submit to the calculations of human greed. Money had to shed its cold shadows on this celestial life and implant a distrust to feelings of the heart in this woman who was all feeling.)

---

12 Balzac, *Eugénie Grandet*, 381.
13 Translation mine.
14 Dostoevskii, *Evgeniia Grande*, 225.

Balzac's opposition between the heart and cold calculations of reason in this excerpt is very important for Dostoevsky's own philosophy and ethics. In Dostoevsky's system of ethical dilemmas that he explores in his novels, the heart is always used as the ultimate criterion for the correct choice when his characters face a difficult decision, whereas the reliance on logical argument alone leads to morally wrong actions.[15] For example, the opposition between the heart and reason is developed in the characters of the two brothers Karamazov. Alyosha is guided by his heart and love for humanity, while Ivan's desire to rely solely on reason causes him to doubt God's existence ultimately leading him to madness.

The last sentence in Dostoevsky's translation of *Eugénie Grandet* sets up a new opposition that is not found in Balzac: between "distrust to feeling" and someone who is "all feeling." Dostoevsky's Evgenia, similar to his most altruistic characters, is guided by her heart rather than reason. But at the same time, the devastating effect of money and her personal experience have taught her to distrust her feelings.

There are also other significant differences that emerge between Balzac's Eugénie and Dostoevsky's Evgenia. For example, Dostoyevsky consistently amplifies the devotional and saintly aspects of Evgenia's personality, so that she is strongly linked to Christian symbolism and Christian ethics. Balzac's description of Eugénie's charitable deeds continues along the following lines: "La main de cette femme panse les plaies secrètes de toutes les familles. Eugénie marche au ciel accompagnée d'un cortège de bienfaits. La grandeur de son âme amoindrit les petitesses de son éducation et les coutumes de sa vie première" (This woman's hand heals the secret wounds in many families. Eugénie proceeds on her way to heaven accompanied by a train of good deeds. The greatness of her soul makes up for the narrowness of her education and the petty habits of her early life).[16]

Dostoevsky's translation, on the other hand, is longer and richer when it comes to Evgenia's devotional qualities. It lacks the touch of levity in Balzac's description:

Тайно рука этой женщины простерта для врачевания ран жизненных.

Она стремится к небу, напутствуемая хором благословений несчастных

---

15 For more on the fallacy of logical reasoning, see Smerdyakov's argument in chapter "Controversy" of *The Brothers Karamazov* requesting the logical proof of God's existence by asking to move a mountain in Fedor Dostoevskii, *Sobranie sochinenii v 12 tomakh* (Moscow, Russia: Azbuka, 1982), vol. 11, 154.

16 Balzac, *Père Goriot, and Eugénie Grandet*, 496.

и слезами благодарности. Великая душа ее уничтожает и покрывает недостатки ее образования и прежние привычки.[17]

(Secretly this woman's hand is stretched out to heal life's wounds. She strives for heaven, accompanied by the chorus of blessings of the unfortunate and by tears of gratitude. Her great soul eliminates and compensates for the shortcomings of her education and her former habits.)

Dostoevsky intensifies the description with the following substitutions: *cortège de bienfaits* becomes "the chorus of blessings of the injured and tears of gratitude." Later in the paragraph Dostoevsky uses two verbs: *уничтожать*—"to eliminate"—and *покрывать*—"to cover, to compensate," whereas Balzac uses only one: *amoindrir*—" to lessen." *Покров* in the Russian Orthodox tradition also means "shroud, cloak" or "protection, intercession" referring to the Virgin Mary's veil that she took off during her prayer for all Christians and unfolded to protect Constantinople from the invasion of pagan armies in the year 910. The protecting veil of the Theotokos and the Feast of the Holy Protectress became one of the most important official Eastern Orthodox Church holidays and has been celebrated since the twelfth century. In Dostoevky's use of *покрывать* one sees again a desire to put greater emphasis on Evgenia's magnanimity and her Christian virtues, further linking her image to the Virgin Mary.

The next sentence in Balzac's text summarizes the fate of Eugénie: "Telle est l'histoire de cette femme, qui n'est pas du monde au milieu du monde; qui, faite pour être magnifiquement épouse et mère, n'a ni mari, ni enfants, ni famille"[18] (Such is the story of this woman, who is in the world but not of it; who, created to be a magnificent wife and mother, has neither husband nor children, nor family).[19]

This is how Dostoevsky renders it: "Вот повесть, вот картина жизни бедного создания, женщины, которая не от мира сего, которая была создана быть нежнейшей супругой и не знала мужа, которая была бы образцом матери и не насладилась счастием иметь детей"[20] (Here is a tale, a picture of the life of a poor creature, a woman, who was not of this world, who was created to be the most tender of spouses and did not know a husband, who would have been an ideal image of a mother and did

---

17 Ibid., 225.
18 Dostoevskii, *Evgeniia Grande*, 381.
19 Balzac, *Père Goriot, and Eugénie Grandet*, 496.
20 Dostoevskii, *Evgeniia Grande*, 225.

not enjoy the happiness of having children). Here, as in previous excerpts, Dostoevsky chose to expand Balzac's original by adding another layer of religious connotation to Evgenia's character. He refers to Evgenia's potential role in life as *образец (obrazets)*—an ideal image or model, here of a mother or a wife. This word is morphologically derived from *obraz*. *Obraz* in the context of the Russian Orthodox tradition means not only an image, but also a "holy image"—as are icons of God, the Virgin Mary, or saints.

These icons occupy a central place in the interior of an Orthodox church and play a prominent role in Orthodox worship and theology. The *obraza* signify the presence of Christ among people and function as a link between heaven and earth. The most frequent figures portrayed as *obraza* are that of Christ and the Virgin Mary, who is viewed in the Russian Orthodox tradition as a human person closest to God. The *obraz* is viewed as a sacred image, a consecrated object, even before the icon itself is created. The painter monks prepare themselves for their task by fasting and penance. Brushes, wood, paint, and all the necessary materials are consecrated before they are used. The painting of an icon is viewed in itself as a liturgical act. Through the icons, the heavenly beings manifest themselves to the congregation and are united with it. According to Ernst Benz,[21] in the Eastern Orthodox Church, the icon is a window that opens into the heavenly world: through it, the believers can see the holy dwellers of Heaven—Christ, the Virgin Mary, and the saints—as well as observe scenes from the Old and New Testament. And through the same window the inhabitants of the celestial world look at ours: hence the need to avoid any improper or indecent behavior: drinking, sexual intercourse, obscene language, violence, and so forth in front of the icons.

Through the use of *obrazets/obraz* Dostoevsky intensifies Evgenia's connection to Heaven. Among other changes, he repeats the opening phrase, adds "and here is the image," which is not in the original, adds "poor creature," changes the three-part rhythm of Balzac's cadence *ni mari, ni enfants, ni famille*, and instead adds a superlative *nezhneishei*—"the most tender." He expands and amplifies Balzac's sentence, building up the sequence of binary oppositions: the most tender of spouses—Evgenia did not know a husband; the model of a mother—she did not enjoy the happiness of having children. These contrasting pairs represent the aesthetics of extreme

---

21 For more details see Ernst Benz, Richard Winston, and Clara Winston, *The Eastern Orthodox Church Its Thought and Life* (Garden City, NJ: Anchor Books, 1963)

polarities that is frequently found in Dostoevsky's novels at all levels: in character description, setting, dialogue, and plot twists.

The last paragraph of the novel compares Eugénie to a Greek statue that has been irretrievably lost at sea: "Parmi les femmes, Eugénie Grandet sera peut-être un type, celui des dévouements jetés à travers les orages du monde et qui s'y engloutissent comme une noble statue enlevée a la Grèce et qui, pendant la transport, tombe à la mer où elle demeurera toujours ignorée"[22] (Among women Eugénie Grandet would perhaps embody the type of devotion that has been thrown through the thunderstorms of the world and is engulfed, as a noble Greek statue during the voyage falls to the bottom of the sea where it will always remain unknown).[23] This unique memorable image of Balzac becomes an expressive metaphor of a beautiful life whose potential was unfulfilled and whose classical beauty is forever lost to the world. Moreover, one of the attributes of the Virgin May is *Stella Maris*—Star of the Sea,[24] a link through which the image of a sea-sunk statue further connects Eugénie to heaven. For unknown reasons, in the subsequent editions of the novel, Balzac considerably shortened the conclusion and this passage was omitted.

Comparing the last paragraphs of Balzac's original and Dostoevsky's translation side by side, one would notice that Dostoevsky again expands the text and makes explicit the connotations that can be only inferred in Balzac's final paragraph. The original text is considerably more laconic and calm, almost understated in its finale.

> В судьбе человеческой жизнь Евгении Гранде может считаться образцом страдальческого самоотвержения, кротко сопротивляющегося людям и поглощенного их бурной, нечистой массой. Она вышла ... как из руки вдохновенного художника Древней Греции выходит божественная статуя; но во время переезда в чужую землю мрамор упадает в море и навеки скрывается от людских восторгов, похвал и удивления.[25]

> (In human fate the life of Evgenia may be considered a model of suffering self-sacrifice, meekly resisting people and absorbed by their turbulent, corrupt mass. She emerged ... as from the hand of inspired artist of Ancient

---

22 Dostoevskii, *Evgeniia Grande*, 384.
23 Translation mine.
24 For more on the history of this term, see "History," St. Mary, Star of the Sea, http://www.stmarylbk.com/History.
25 Dostoevskii, *Evgeniia Grande*, 266.

Greece there appears a divine statue; but during the journey to a foreign land the marble falls into the sea and hides forever from human admiration, praise, and amazement.)

Here Dostoevsky, as he did regularly in his own writing later, creates a strong system of contrasts. He emphasizes the opposition between Evgenia's purity and the corruption (*нечистый*) of the world. He also adds here the epithet "divine" (*божественный*), accentuating again Evgenia's connection to Heaven and to God's virtues. Dostoevsky changed Balzac's passive participle *ignorée* and instead made the verb construction active. Replacing the passive construction with the active makes the text more dynamic, so that the statue is treated as an animate object. This strengthens the association between Evgenia and the statue, with the metaphor of the statue lost at sea representing her lost life. Dostoevsky also expands the last sentence adding that (the statue) "is hiding from people's admiration, praise, and amazement." The motif of hiding one's inner feelings and emotions from the world will become very prominent in Dostoevsky's own writings. The inability to communicate and connect with others despite a passionate desire to forge a connection or a personal relationship is at the center of the *Notes from the Underground* (1864) and is at the root of the personal tragedy of the pawnbroker in *The Meek One* (1876). Here, in Dostoevsky's translation of the conclusion of *Eugénie Grandet*, the essential Dostoevsky motif of alienation, emotional detachment, and being misunderstood by the world appears for the first time.

The Concept of Meek Suffering in "The Meek One" (1876)

In the final paragraph of his translation, Dostoevsky departs from the original text to connect the two seemingly opposing notions and create a salient image of meek resistance (*кроткое сопротивление*) that will later become very important to his own aesthetics. For the young Dostoevsky, these words hold a rich symbolic and theological meaning. We will analyze the significance of this concept of meekness in greater detail in the context of Dostoevsky's own beliefs and in the broader frame of Russian Orthodox tradition.

Dostoevsky uses the adjective "meek" (*кроткая*) in the title of his very well-known story "The Meek One." This epithet brings into focus the main quality of his central character. "The Meek One" is a tragic story of a tormented passionate relationship between two lonely and strong-willed people—a young innocent girl and a proud pawnbroker who, in his own words, "takes revenge upon society." The pawnbroker marries the young woman and tries to completely suppress her will and individuality by responding to her love with silence, coldness, and sternness. The marriage quickly turns into a confrontation. At the turning point of the novella the young wife even tries to shoot her husband with his revolver, but her innocence and moral purity prevent her from going through with the murder. After that episode, the pawnbroker says triumphantly: "I won, and she was forever defeated." Ultimately, the "meek one" is unable to continue living with her callous husband and she throws herself out of the window, clutching the icon of Mother of God to her breast. After her death, the proud pawnbroker is plunged into despair and he understands all too well that he drove his wife to suicide by his coldness and pride, and his inability to make human commections was the cause of her tragedy. He realizes that he waited too long to express his feelings but at this point it is too late and her life is lost.

This short story encompasses many of Dostoevsky's important themes that are also present in his great novels. There is a male character who is extremely proud and lonely, disillusioned, embittered, and unable to open up to others and to love fully. His foil is an idealistic and innocent young woman who at first wants to give her husband all the love in her heart but is ultimately crushed by his indifference and moral cruelty. Despite her youth and outward physical fragility, the female character has moral supremacy over her older cynical husband. She is not willing to compromise her principles and chooses death over life with the person that she is no longer able to accept as a husband.

Significantly, the female character of "The Meek One" remains unnamed throughout the text. She is only known by her defining quality. For the readers, this is enough to create a poignant image, because the concept of meekness is very important for Orthodox theological thought, as will be shown below. Her adversary and the narrator of the story, the proud pawnbroker, also has no name. This lowly occupation would not have been expected from a person of a noble social standing. He is a member of the nobility, but he was thrown out of his regiment after refusing to fight a duel to defend its honor. His primary motivation is to avenge himself against the entire world for what he perceives as the unfair treatment given to him by his peers, and for all the harsh realities of homeless life that he experienced in Saint Petersburg after his departure from the army. Similarly to Balzac, Dostoevsky viewed the figure of a pawnbroker as a symbolic incarnation of evil, representing the hidden power of money over human lives, and the absence of compassion for human suffering. Thus, from the very beginning of his story, Dostoevsky sets up the binary opposition of conflicting human values: Christian virtue represented by the "meek one" and cold calculations of capital represented by the pawnbroker.

Leaving the main characters nameless is an interesting choice, because names are very important in literature. Balzac, for example, places a great emphasis on names; even the titles of his novels frequently contain only the names of the main characters: *Eugénie Grandet, Cousine Bette, Cousin Pons, Duchesse de Langeais, César Birotteau,* and so forth. Dostoevsky also frequently uses characters' names for titles of his works (*Netochka Nezvanova, The Brothers Karamazov, Mr. Prokharchin*). He also follows the literary tradition of giving the characters names that would signify their salient features. For example, Raskolnikov's surname is derived from the word *raskol*—the term for the famous seventeenth-century schism in the Russian Orthodox Church between the Old Believers who followed the old customs in church service and the New Believers who accepted the reforms of Patriarch Nikon calling for alignment of Russian liturgy with the Greek one. As a result, many of the Old Believers who protested against these reforms were captured and lost their lives by being murdered or burned alive. The echoes of this terrible time can be felt in many of the celebrated Russian artistic works of the nineteenth century, such as Modest Mussorgsky's opera *Khovanschina*, which describes the period of the schism. Thus, Raskolnikov's last name alludes to the famous split in Russian Orthodox Church, and at the same time indicates a psychological conflict: he is a person wth a "split soul," plagued by a moral dilemma about the right to murder another human being. Other Dostoevsky's characters also have names that convey to the readers their moral and spiritual worth, for example, Sonya (a diminutive of Sophia, which in Greek means "wisdom") and Razumikhin (from the Russian verb *razumet'*—"to understand") in *Crime and Punishment*, or Smerdyakov (from theRussian verb *smerdet'*—"to have a foul smell") in *The Brothers Karamazov*.

In *The Meek One*, as well, most secondary characters have names that carry important connotations about the characters themselves. The main characters' only household servant is named Lukeria. This name is a version of Glikeria, which is derived from a Greek word meaning "sweet."[26] The attributes associated with this name are honesty and adherence to principles.[27] In Turgenev's short story "The Living Relic" (1873) the female protagonist, a peasant woman Lukeria, also has the ability to foresee the coming events, and she predicts her own death. In Dostoevsky's story, Lukeria becomes a witness to the tragedy in the house of the pawnbroker and his psychologically tormented relationship with his wife. It is significant that after the wife's suicide, Lukeria decides to quit her position at the pawnbroker's house, thus silently accusing him of her mistress's death despite his protests. A business partner of the pawnbroker is named Dobronravov, an ironic name that means "good-natured."

However, Dostoevsky does not overuse this device: there are also names in the story that do not seem to convey any information about the characters. The pawnbroker's other business partner is called Moser, a surname that is not important in itself and merely alludes to the fact that many pawnbrokers in Saint Petersburg were Jewish. Then, the pawnbroker's rival in the regiment and his greatest enemy is known only by his patronymic— Yefimovich. The lack of identifying details, which Yefimovich shares with the main characters, makes it possible to read their story as a parable applicable for all times and places.

Dostoevsky's readers would immediately be guided towards such universalist reading by the title of the story, with its rich religious subtext. The word "meekness" (*krotkost'*) in Russian Orthodox tradition is a rendering of the Greek πραότητα,[28] which has a meaning of gentleness, sweetness, attentiveness, or courteousness. It also implies great self-control, self-restraint, and strength of spirit. These manifold connotations of meekness are found already in the Scriptures, in which the word is used to describe the martyrs who have demonstrated great strength of spirit under extraordinary circumstances of hardship.

In the Russian Orthodox tradition, and in Chistianity in general, meekness is considered a valuable virtue associated with great spiritual fortitude. This is reflected in Christ's statement "Blessed are the meek, for they shall inherit the earth."[29] In Russian this Biblical phrase has exactly the same word as the title of Dostoevsky's story: "Блаженны кроткие,

---

26 See "Znachenie imeni Liker'ia," Kakzovut.ru, http://kakzovut.ru/names/lukeriya.html.

27 Ibid.

28 See "πραότητα," Almaany English-Greek Dictionary, www.almaany.com.

29 King James Bible, Matthew 5:5.

ибо они наследуют землю."[30] In this passage meekness is viewed as the ability to fully submit to God, maintaining inner peace and contentment, self-possession and resistance to provocations. The meek are able to maintain silence in the face of an insult rather then give in to an outburst of anger. This statement from the New Testament presents a stark contrast to the Old Testament maxim "An eye for an eye, a tooth for tooth" where retaliation and forceful response were the norm.

Meekness as a virtue is mentioned many times in the Bible in various circumstances and contexts. For example, in the Second Epistle of Paul to Corinthians, preparing the Corinthians for his arrival, Paul describes himself as meek: "Now I, Paul myself, beseech you by the meekness and gentleness of Christ, who in presence am base among you, but being absent am bold toward you."[31] Here the two seemingly opposite qualities—meekness and boldness—are connected in one person. Following Paul's statement, Christian theology views meekness as a manifestation of inner strength and firmness. Another religious leader, Moses, is also described as meek: "Now the man Moses was very meek, above all the men who were upon the face of the Earth."[32] In this citation meekness as modesty and self-effacing qualities of the soul are viewed as great spiritual assets and attributes of a great man and spiritual leader.

The *Encyclopedic Dictionary of the Bible* emphasizes fortitude and self-control as an essential part of meekness: "Особенные действия христианской кротости состоят в том, чтобы не роптать не только на Бога, но и на людей, когда происходит что-либо противное нашим желаниям, не предаваться гневу, не превозноситься"[33] (Particular acts of Christian humility consist in not only rebelling against God, but also against people when something goes against our wishes, not to indulge in anger, not to be haughty). In Russian Orthodox tradition many more references to meekness in the context of the Bible can be found.[34]

---

30 See Azbuka very, http://azbyka.ru/biblia/.

31 King James Bible, Second Epistle to Corintheans 10:2.

32 King James Bible, Numbers 12:3.

33 *Illiustrirovannaia Bibleiskaia entsiklopediia Arkhimandrita Nikofora* (Moscow, Russia: Eksmo, 2015); "Krotkost'," dic.academic.ru/dic.nsf/biblerus/65803/Кроткость.

34 For example, Saint Ignatius Brenchaninov gives the following definition of meekness: "Кротость—смиренная преданность Богу, соединенная с верой и осененная Божественной благодатью, покорность сердца уму" (Meekness is humble devotion to God, united with faith and blessed by the divine grace, submission of heart to mind). Supporting the Russian Orthodox view of meekness as highly desirable to cultivate,

Thus, meekness in Russian Christian theology and in Dostoevsky's system of values becomes the signifier not of weakness of character but, on the contrary, of inner strength derived from a person's deep faith in God. For the young Dostoevsky, the image of Balzac's Eugénie becomes a tragic and lofty symbol of "meek" suffering. He returns to this image of a suffering, self-sacrificing noble woman again and again throughout his literary career. The next sections of this chapter trace and discuss manifold textual echoes and connections between Dostoevsky's interpretation of Balzac's Eugénie and his own ideal female characters.

Portrayal of Alexandra Mikhailovna in Netochka Nezvanova (1849)

An early example of a meek suffering woman, who lives in unhappiness and loneliness with the cherished memories of lost love, is Alexandra Mikhailovna, a character from Dostoevsky's unfinished novel *Netochka Nezvanova* (1849). This novel was written seven years after Dostoevsky had finished his translation of *Eugénie Grandet*, and the character of Alexandra Mikhailovna, with her loveless marriage and her lost love, shows many reflections of Balzac's Eugénie's tragic loneliness. The contrast between Alexandra Mikhailovna's past love and her present spiritual solitude echoes the fate of Evgenia.

Alexandra Mikhailovna is a wealthy noblewoman, kind, loving, and generous, who is trapped in an unhappy marriage with a cold older man. She takes a poor orphan, Netochka, into her home and raises her as her own child. Young Netochka, the narrator of the story, becomes aware early on of a hidden tension existing between the beautiful and mysterious Alexandra Mikhailovna and her distant unapproachable husband. Like many of Dostoevsky's children, young Netochka is very observant and precocious, and she senses that in Alexandra Mikhailovna's past lies a tragic secret that cast a dark shadow on her unhappy life with her husband. This is how Netochka describes her benefactor:

> Характер ее был робок, слаб. Смотря на ясные, спокойные черты лица ее, нельзя было предположить с первого раза, чтоб какая-нибудь тревога могла смутить ее праведное сердце. Помыслить нельзя было, чтоб она могла не любить хоть кого-нибудь; сострадание всегда

Russian saint Cyril of Turov instructed the believers not to search for wisdom, but search for meekness instead.

брало в ее душе верх даже над самим отвращением, а между тем она привязана была к немногим друзьям и жила в полном уединении. . . . Она была страстна и впечатлительна по натуре своей, но в то же время как будто сама боялась своих впечатлений, как будто каждую минуту стерегла свое сердце, не давая ему забыться, хотя бы в мечтанье. Иногда вдруг, среди самой светлой минуты, я замечала слезы в глазах ее: словно внезапное тягостное воспоминание чего-то мучительно терзавшего ее совесть вспыхивало в ее душе; как будто что-то стерегло ее счастье и враждебно смущало его. И чем, казалось, счастливее была она, чем покойнее, яснее была минута ее жизни, тем ближе была тоска, тем вероятнее была внезапная грусть, слезы: как будто на нее находил припадок. Я не запомню ни одного спокойного месяца в целые восемь лет. Муж, по-видимому, очень любил ее; она обожала его. Но с первого взгляда казалось, как будто что-то было недосказано между ними. Какая-то тайна была в судьбе ее; по крайней мере я начала подозревать с первой минуты. . . .[35]

(Hers was a frail and timid nature. Looking at the clear, calm features of her face, one would never have imagined that any anxiety could have troubled her virtuous heart. It was unthinkable that she should be without love for anyone; compassion was always uppermost in her soul, prevailing even over revulsion, and yet she had few attachments and lived in complete seclusion. Though sensitive and of a passionate temperament, she seemed to be afraid of her own feelings; it was as though she constantly stood guard over her emotions, never giving them free rein even in dreams. Sometimes in her brightest moments I would suddenly notice tears in her eyes, as if the poignant memory of something that fretted and preyed on her conscience had unexpectedly flared up in her heart, or as if something was keeping watch over her happiness and maliciously disturbed it. It seemed that the happier she was and the calmer and more serene her life, the more likely her sudden melancholy and tears, as though this made her susceptible to an attack. I can recall not a single undisturbed month during those eight years. Her husband evidently loved her very much, and she adored him. But it seemed to me that there was something unspoken between them, some mystery in her life, or so I had begun to suspect from the very first.)[36]

---

35 Dostoevskii, *Sobranie sochinenii v 12 tomakh*, 1:326.
36 Fyodor Dostoyevsky, *Netochka Nezvanova* (Englewood Cliffs, NJ: Prentice-Hall, 1970), 137.

Common spiritual qualities central to Dostoevsky's concept of an ideal woman are found in his descriptions of Evgenia[37] and of Alexandra Mikhailovna[38]—depth of feeling, sincerity, compassion, serenity of spirit, and the ability to love passionately, despite adversity. The word that Dostoevsky chooses to characterize the beauty of Alexandra's face is *ясность*—this word in Russian in its first direct meaning is translated as "clarity" but also has the additional meanings of serenity and lucidity. In Dostoevsky's portrayal of Evgenia seven years prior, he uses exactly the same adjectives, saying that her features were clear and light (*черты лица ее были ясны и светлы*).[39] There is also a spiritual dimension to the lucidity of Evgenia's face, which has the ability to sooth spiritual anguish (*эти черты покоили взор ваш; вся душа покорялась ей, и от нее же принимала эту ясность, это спокойствие духа*). Ясность ума—clarity of mind—is also a quality highly valued in the Russian Orthodox tradition; Orthodox priests recommend that their parishioners pray to attain this ability, since it would protect them from wrong actions. In Dostoevsky's poetics, clarity of mind and serenity of spirit can only be attained through deep religious faith in the face of adverse circumstances.

In close study of Dostoevsky's descriptions of both Evgenia and Alexandra, one finds numerous allusions to heaven and religious virtue. For example, Evgenia's features are "bathed in heavenly light"—*облитые райским светом*, and she has "a celestial radiance of Madonna"—*небесное сияние Мадонны*.[40] Alexandra's glance is "righteously calm"—*праведно-спокойный*, and she demonstrates a lot of childlike faith—*столько младенческого верования*.[41] Religious connotations appear in both descriptions, and the readers can perceive that it is very important for Dostoevsky's system of moral values. In his own later works Dostoevsky constantly returns to his belief that deep religious faith protects moral purity. This notion of righteous moral life was already very much at the center of his attention even while he was working on the Balzac translation.

---

37 Dostoevskii, *Evgeniia Grande*, 68.
38 Idem, *Sobranie sochinenii v 12 tomakh*, 1:326.
39 Idem, *Evgeniia Grande*, 68.
40 Ibid., 68.
41 Dostoevskii, *Sobranie sochinenii v 12 tomakh*, 1:326.

The Portrait of Sophia in The Raw Youth *(1875)*

The spiritual and moral qualities that young Dostoevsky brought into his interpretation of Balzac's Eugénie consistently reappear in Dostoevsky's own images of ideal women that he created later in his novels. The salient features of selfless love, inner strength, moral purity, and deep religious faith, which allow the female character to accept suffering and forgive, find their incarnation in Sonya in *Crime and Punishment* (1866), in Alyosha's mother in *The Brothers Karamazov* (1880), and in another Sonya, Arkady's mother in *The Raw Youth* (1875).

In his novels, Dostoevsky frequently introduces the opposition of a visually striking female beauty, which leads a man into temptation, and plainer appearance that hides the quiet charm of a deeply virtuous woman. For Dostoevsky's aesthetics and morality, flamboyant female beauty is associated with danger, passion, and sin, as is evident in the portrayal of Nastasya Fillipovna in *The Idiot* (1869). On the contrary, a more ordinary, reserved appearance, whose attractiveness can only be felt by the chosen few upon a closer acquaintance, for Dostoevsky is aligned with moral righteousness and inner goodness. Dostoevsky's own personal experience of a turbulent love affair with "an infernal beauty" Appolinnaria Suslova and his later marriage to his stenographer Anna Snitkina seems to fit into this model. Many years after their marriage, Anna wrote in her memoirs that although she was not a beautiful woman, Dostoevsky felt that her moral qualities shone like "a prized diamond"[42] and that he esteemed them more than anything else. She also recalls that when he proposed to her, Dostoevsky made up a fictional story about an ageing artist and a young girl with whom the artist fell in love. According to Anna's memoirs, the young girl had all the qualities that Dostoevsky admired in women—she was meek, intelligent, kind, vivacious and tactful:

> Аня была кротка, умна, добра, жизнерадостна и обладала большим тактом в сношениях с людьми. Придавая в те годы большое значение женской красоте, я не удержалась и спросила: "А хороша собой ваша героиня?"—"Не красавица, конечно, но очень недурна. Я люблю ее лицо."[43]

---

42 Anna Dostoevskaia, *Vospominaniia 1846–1917: Solntse moei zhizni, Fedor Dostoevskii* (Moscow, Russia: Boslen, 2015), 133.

43 Ibid.

(Anya was meek, intelligent, kind, vivacious, and possessed great tact in personal relationships. Attaching great importance to women's beauty in those years, I could not resist asking:

—Is your personage good-looking?

—She is not beautiful, certainly, but not bad-looking. I love her face.)[44]

From this fictional portrait of an ideal woman, the reader can derive a sense of what Dostoevsky was looking for in the one he would make his wife. This dialogue shows the same opposition that emerges between conventional beauty, easily recognized by society, and a quiet charm, esteemed by only few. It is worth noting that meekness is placed first in the list of female virtues, taking precedence over intelligence and kindness.

In keeping with the dichotomy of outward beauty versus inner goodness, Dostoevsky's most altruistic female characters are not necessarily beautiful from the conventional point of view, but they all possess that calm inner radiance manifesting spiritual peace and serenity that is only attainable by a certain type of person. This can be seen many times in the descriptions of female characters in his later works. The antecedent to this notion of an easy pleasing beauty seen by everyone vs. inner goodness shining through the eyes and only perceptible by the chosen few can be found in Balzac's description of Eugénie. In the beginning of the novel Balzac gives his readers a physical portrait of Eugénie after her first meeting with her dashing Parisian cousin Charles who enchants her with his looks and fashionable clothes and with whom she falls deeply in love. Balzac describes Eugenie in detail when she gets up early in the morning, gets dressed, and is caught in a reverie by the window:

> Eugénie, grande et forte, n'avait donc rien de *joli*; elle était belle de cette beauté si facile à méconnaître, et que saisit seulement l'artiste. Mais le peintre qui cherche ici-bas le type de la céleste pureté de Marie, qui demande à toute la nature féminine ces yeux fiers et modestes, devinés par Raphael, ces lignes vierges que donne parfois la nature, mais que la chasteté dans la vie et la pensée peut seule conserver ou faire acquérir, ce peintre amoureux d'un si rare modèle, eût trouvé tout à coup dans le visage d'Eugénie la noblesse innée qui s'ignore; il eût vu sous un front calme, un monde d'amour; et, dans la coupe de yeux, dans l'habitude des paupières, le *je ne sais quoi* divin. Ses traits, les contours de sa tête, que l'expression n'a jamais ni altérés, ni

---

44 Translation mine.

fatigués, ressemblaient aux lignes d'horizon si doucement tranchées dans le lointain des lacs tranquilles. Cette physionomie calme, colorée, bordée de lueur comme une jolie fleur fraiche éclose, reposait l'âme, et communiquait le charme de la conscience qui s'y reflétait; elle redemandait les regards.[45]

(Eugénie, tall and sturdy, had nothing of the prettiness which appeals to the masses; but she had that true beauty so easy not to recognize, which only the artist fully appreciates. The painter who seeks in this world a model with the heavenly purity of the Virgin, who looks among all womankind for these modestly proud eyes divined by Raphael, those virginal lines, often inborn, but which only a chaste and Christian life can either preserve or bestow—such a painter, in love with his ideal, would suddenly have discovered in Eugénie's face that nobility which is unaware of itself; between her clam brow he would have sensed a world of love, and in the shape of her eyes and the lowering of her eyelids a suggestion of the divine. Her features, the outlines of her face, neither altered nor wearied by passion, resembled the vague contours of a gentle and distant horizon glimpsed across tranquil lakes. This calm and rosy countenance, haloed with light like a lovely, full-blown flower, was refreshing to the soul, distilled the charm of the spirit reflected in it, and held the attention.)[46]

Dostoevsky makes several subtle changes to this portrait:

Конечно, свет не признал бы Евгению красавицей, но мощная, величественная красота ее была бы достойно оценена художником. Если он ищет на земле небесного сияния Мадонны, если он ищет тех величественно-скромных очей, которые постиг Рафаэль, тех светлых девственных контуров, которые сохраняются лишь в огне целомудрия тела и мысли, если художник влюблен в этот почти небесный идеал свой, то жадный взор его умел бы открыть в чертах Евгении многое, что осуществило бы заветные мечты его. Эти черты, блистающие свежестью, на которых еще не дохнуло пресыщение тлетворным дыханием своим, эти черты были ясны и светлы, как тихий край горизонта, окаймляющий вдали зеркальную поверхность необозримого озера. Эти черты, безмятежные, облитые райским светом, покоили взор ваш, утишали в сердце вашем неистовые порывы желания и смиряли душу.

---

45 Balzac, *Eugénie Grandet*, 132.
46 Balzac, *Père Goriot, and Eugénie Grandet*, 351.

(Of course, society would not consider Eugenia beautiful, but her powerful, majestic beauty would be properly appreciated by an artist. If he is looking for the celestial radiance of the Madonna on Earth, if he seeks those majestic modest eyes that Raphael comprehended, those bright pristine contours, which are preserved only in the fire of chastity of the body and thought, if an artist is in love with his almost heavenly ideal, then his voracious eyes could discover in Evgenia's features much that would fulfill his cherished dreams. These features, sparkling with freshness, not yet touched by a corrupting breath of satiety, these features were clear and bright, like the quiet edge of the horizon, bordering the immense mirror-like surface of the lake. These features, serene, bathed in heavenly light, rested your eyes, calmed violent impulses of desire in your heart and humbled the soul.)[47]

Dostoevsky omits the attributive adjectives that Balzac chose to describe Eugénie—*grande et forte* (tall and a little heavy-set)—and instead emphasizes Evgenia's "powerful, majestic beauty." Overall, he focuses on the metaphorical meaning rather than creating an exact physical description. Furthermore, in his portrait of Eugénie, Balzac creates an opposition between *joli* and *belle* (*elle n'avait rien de joli, mais elle était belle*). There is an important difference between the meanings of these words. The Larousse dictionary gives the following definitions: "*joli—dont la vue procurement le plaisir, de l'agrément, qui séduit par sa grâce, son charme*" (*joli*—whose sight procures pleasure, which seduces by its grace, its charm) and "*belle—qui suscite un plaisir esthétique d'ordre visuel ou auditif; qui suscite un sentiment admiratif par sa superiorité intellectuelle, morale ou physique*" (*belle*—that which arouses an aesthetic pleasure of visual or auditory order; that arouses a feeling of admiration by its intellectual, moral, or physical superiority).[48] This fine distinction between *joli*—easy, visually pleasing beauty—and *belle*, a higher, more abstract concept of beauty frequently tied to moral perfection, is significant for the French language and for Balzac's aesthetics. Unfortunately, this opposition could not be replicated in Russian, so Dostoevsky left it out entirely. He did the same with Balzac's comment about Eugénie's beauty being the type that is so easy not to recognize. Instead, the translation says that Evgenia had that type of beauty that could

---

47 Translation mine.
48 *Dictionnaires Larousse français monolingue et bilingues en ligne*, Larousse, January 1, 2011, https://www.larousse.fr/dictionnaires/francais; translation mine.

only be appreciated fully by a certain type of an artist, who is looking for the celestial ideal and virginal modesty of Raphael's Madonna.

This substitution is representative of the way Dostoevsky endows the portrait of Evgenia with several attributes typically used in describing saints that are not in Balzac's original. He writes that her facial features are "bathed in heavenly light" (*черты, облитые райским светом*), he grants Evgenia the ability to soothe the eyes of those who gaze upon her, calm violent outbursts of desire in human heart, and humble the soul. The capacity of eyes to comfort the soul and to admire God can be also seen in the writings of the Russian Orthodox Church, for example, those of Saint Efrem Sirin.[49] This description shows that young Dostoevsky already equated beauty with divine goodness, which became a cornerstone of his aesthetics later.

In Dostoevsky's later novel *The Raw Youth* (1875), one of his major five novels (the other four are *Crime and Punishment, The Idiot, The Devils,* and *Brothers Karamazov*), we find the same image of a modest self-sacrificing woman who is not conventionally beautiful but who is nonetheless altruistic and able to love deeply and passionately. These traits are embodied in the character of Sophia Andreevna, the mother of Arkady, the titular character and the narrator of the novel. This is how Arkady describes his mother's appearance:

> Я знаю, однако же, наверно, что иная женщина обольщает красотой своей, или тем, чем знает, в тот же миг; другую же надо полгода разжевывать, прежде чем понять, что в ней есть; и чтобы рассмотреть такую и влюбиться, то мало смотреть и мало быть готовым на что угодно, а надо быть, сверх того, чем—то еще одаренным. . . . Я знаю из нескольких рук положительно, что мать моя красавицей не была, хотя тогдашнего портрета ее, который где-то есть, я не видал. С первого взгляда в нее влюбиться, стало быть, нельзя было.[50]

> (I know, however, for sure that one woman seduces with her beauty, or by what she knows, in an instant; for another woman it takes you half a year to study her closely before you understand what it is she has; and in order to distinguish it and fall in love, it is not enough to see and be ready for anything, but moreover, you have to be especially gifted. . . . I know positively

---

49 *Tvoreniia sviatogo prepodobnogo Efrema Sirina,* https://svyatye.com.

50 Dostoevskii, *Sobranie sochinenii v 15 tomakh,* 9: 224.

from several sources that my mother was not a beauty, but then I have not seen her portrait, which is somewhere there. . . . Therefore, one could not fall in love with her at first glance.)[51]

In this passage, there is a direct textual echo of Dostoevsky's description of Balzac's Evgenia, where the narrator says that although Evgenia is not a beauty in the conventional sense of the word, her charm can be appreciated by a sensitive artist. Similarly, the narrator of *The Raw Youth* stresses that the quiet beauty of Sophia is only recognized fully after a long period of knowing her and is not something that can be noticed at first sight.

Dostoevsky's Sophia Andreevna shares with Evgenia not only her quiet type of beauty, but also her tragic fate of unhappy love. From the recollections of Arkady, her illegitimate son, the reader learns that young Sophia had fallen in love with a rich landowner, Versilov. Although she was married to another man, she had his illegitimate child, and their love affair continued for many years. The dashing Versilov was frequently absent from her life, he fell in love multiple times, and even proposed to other women. This conventional story of a poor girl seduced by a rich nobleman bears some similarities to the plot of Balzac's novel, but Dostoevsky's treatment of this topic is very different from Balzac's. One example can be found in Balzac's *Lost Illusions* and *Splendor and Misery of the Courtesans*. In these novels the readers are introduced to a tragic story of La Torpille, whose real name is Esther Gobseck. She becomes a glamorous courtesan in Paris and later falls in love with Lucien de Rubampre, a protagonist in both of these novels. In the end Esther commits suicide so that she can break free from her relationship with Baron de Nucingen and this is the catastrophic finale of her life. In Dostoevsky's novel the story of Sophia and Versilov has a happier ending. Sophia loves Versilov and continues to love him all her life despite his outbursts of anger and multiple affairs with other women. Her constancy and selfless love lead him to a deep spiritual transformation and bring him back to her in the end of the novel.

In one of the episodes of the novel, Arkady sees a photograph of his mother on Versilov's desk and is stunned to notice Versilov's face changing when he looks at the portrait. For Versilov, similar to Sophia, this love is something special that he carries throughout his turbulent life. He even compares Sophia to an angel to whom he would always come back. Arkady recalls that "Я оглянулся на него и был поражен выражением его лица.

---

51 Translation mine.

Он был несколько бледен, но с горячим, напряженным взглядом, сиявшим как бы счастием и силой; такого выражения я еще не знал у него вовсе.—Я не знал, что вы так любите маму!"[52] (I looked at him and was struck by the expression on his face. He was a little pale, but with a hot, intense look, as if radiating happiness and strength; such an expression I did not previously know in him at all.—I did not know that you love my mother so much!).[53] Versilov looks at the photo of Sophia and continues: "Здесь же, в этом портрете, солнце, как нарочно, застало Соню в ее главном мгновении—стыдливой, кроткой любви и несколько дикого, пугливого ее целомудрия. Да и счастлива же была она тогда, когда наконец убедилась, что я так жажду иметь ее портрет!"[54] (Here, in this portrait, the sun, as if on purpose, caught Sonya in her most important moment—of bashful, meek love and somewhat savage, timid chastity. Yes, and how happy she was when she was finally convinced that I so yearn to have her portrait!).[55] Just as for Balzac, for Dostoevsky the highest point of a woman's life is her self-sacrifice for love, and this is emphasized in the description of Sophia. The idea of meekness present in Sophia's portrait and its manifold connotations for Dostoevsky's poetics have been discussed earlier in the chapter, but the second shared element—that of chastity—is equally significant.

When young Dostoevsky began to work on Balzac's text, he used the adjective *целомудренный* (chaste) in several places in describing Evgenia. The concept of *целомудрие* (chastity) is one of the key categories for Dostoevsky's moral code and it is also very important for the Russian Orthodox Church. In Russian Orthodoxy, the notion of chastity goes beyond physical aspects and implies purity of body and soul, of thoughts and actions, moral integrity, and nobility of character. The *Biblical Encyclopedia of Brokgauz* defines the concept of *целомудрие* as "цельность характера и чистота движущих мотивов, искренность помыслов и чувств"[56] (integrity of character and purity of motives, sincerity in thoughts and feelings.)[57] The corresponding Greek word is σωφροσύνη,[58] referencing

---

52 Dostoevskii, *Sobranie sochinenii v 15 tomakh*, 10:271.

53 Translation mine.

54 Dostoevskii, *Sobranie sochinenii v 15 tomakh*, 10:271.

55 Translation mine.

56 *Bibleiskaiia Entsiklopediia Brokgauza*, https://bible-facts.org/bibleyskaya-enciklopediya-c-.html.

57 Translation mine.

58 "Tselomudrie," https://azbyka.ru/tselomudrie.

the ancient Greek concept of soundness of mind, prudence, temperance, discretion, and self-control.[59] The notion opposite to chastity is depravity—*разврат*. In Dostoevsky's great novels, a binary opposition between the characters leading a chaste and moral life and their antagonists submerged in depravity and corruption is frequently used to create a strong conflict in the plot and to continue emotional tension in the narrative.

Unlike Dostoevsky's translation, Balzac's novel is not focused on the manifold Christian connotations of chastity and depravity that are so important to Dostoevsky. Instead, in Balzac's Eugénie one can see more secular attributes, centered on the general moral aspects of her character: *pure* (innocent), *ange de pureté* (angel of purity), or the noun *la candeur* (clarity, candor), which is placed quite far semantically from chastity, and represents a completely different character interpretation. *Dictionnaire de l'Académie française*[60] lists several meanings for *la candeur* that evolved throughout the centuries. Its original meaning, derived from its etymology, is that of whiteness: *blancheur éclatante, très pure*, the second meaning is that of purity of the soul, manifested by simple and sincere conduct: *pureté de l'âme qui se manifeste par un comportement simple et sincère*. The third meaning is that of an innocent heart of a person without life experience: *innocence de cœur d'une personne sans expérience de la vie*. When Balzac chose this word to characterize Eugénie's behavior with Charles, he clearly had in mind all these connotations, since the character of Eugénie corresponds to all shades of the meaning of *candeur*. Dostoevsky replaced this word with something quite different—"chaste charm"—*целомудренная прелесть*.[61]

Candeur in Russian is frequently translated as *чистосердечие* (lit. "purity of the heart") or *простодушие* (lit. "simplicity of the soul"). Many of Dostoevsky's ideal meek women and precocious children possess this quality. For example, the central character of *The Meek One* has the innocence of youth when she first meets the pawnbroker, as does Sonya from *Crime and Punishment*. When Raskolnikov comes to her room before she reads the Lazarus story to him, he is amazed that she managed to keep her purity of the spirit (чистоту духа) so far: "'But can it be true?' he exclaimed to himself. 'Can it be that this being, who

59 Henry George Liddell and Robert Scott, *A Greek-English Lexicon*. (Oxford, UK: Clarendon Press, 1940) http://www.perseus.tufts.edu.

60 "Candeur," La-definition, http://www.la-definition.fr/definition/candeur.

61 Dostoevskii, *Evgeniia Grande*, 151.

has still kept her purity of spirit, in the end will be consciously pulled into this vile, stinking hole?'"[62] The purity of spirit or soul is shared by Dostoevsky's noblest characters. It guards them against the corruption and sordidness of daily life.

Dostoevsky makes his Evgenia not only innocent and pure but chaste, stressing her goodness and connection to God. He minimizes and in some instances omits altogether Balzac's allusions to sensual pleasures of love, as illustrated in the following example in one of the key scenes of the novel when Eugénie and Charles exchange vows and he kisses her breast:

> Quand Eugénie mis la clef dans son sein, elle n'eut pas le courage de défendre à Charles d'en baiser la place.
>
> —Elle n'en sortira pas de là, mon ami.
>
> —Hé, bien, mon amour, mon coeur y sera toujours aussi.
>
> —Ah! Charles, ce n'est pas bien,—dit-elle d'un accent peu grondeur.
>
> —Ne sommes nous pas mariés, répondit-il, j'ai ta parole, prends la mienne.
>
> —A toi, pour jamais! Fut dit deux fois de part et d'autre.
>
> Acune promesse faite sur cette terre ne fit plus pure, la candeur d'Eugénie avait momentanément sanctifié l'amour de Charles.[63]

> (When Eugénie put the key in her bosom, she had not the courage to prevent Charles from kissing the spot.
>
> "It shall never leave that place, my dear."
>
> "Then my heart will always be there too."
>
> "Oh, Charles, you mustn't," she said chidingly.
>
> "Are we not married?" he replied. "I have your promise, accept mine."
>
> "I am yours forever!" They each said, repeating the words twice over.
>
> No promise made upon this earth was ever more pure, Eugénie's innocence had momentarily sanctified the young man's love.)[64]

This excerpt has some significant textual changes and omissions in Dostoevsky's translation:

---

62 Fyodor Dostoevsky, *Crime and Punishment: A Novel in Six Parts with Epilogue*, trans. Richard Pevear and Larissa Volokhonsky (New York: Vintage, 1993), 323.

63 Balzac, *Eugénie Grandet*, 262.

64 Idem, *Père Goriot, and Eugénie Grandet*, 427.

Когда Евгения спрятала ключ на грудь свою, она не могла воспрепятствовать Шарлю поцеловать место его теперешнего хранилища.

—Здесь ему место, друг мой.

—Вместе с моим сердцем, отвечал Шарль.

—Ах, братец, братец!—тоном упрека прошептала Евгения.

—Разве мы уже не соединены, моя возлюбленная? ты дала мне свое слово, возьми же и мое.

—Навсегда! Навсегда!

Два раза с обеих сторон было произнесено это торжественное слово, и ни один обет не мог быть ни чище, ни святее этого. Целомудренная прелесть Евгении освятила и любовь Шарля.[65]

(When Evgenia hid the key on her bosom, she could not prevent Charles from kissing the place of its present storage.

—Here it will stay, my friend.

—With my heart,—answered Charles.

—Ah! Cousin, cousin!—Evgenia whispered in a reproaching tone.

—Are we not already joined, my beloved? You gave me your word, take mine.

—Forever! Forever!

That solemn word was uttered twice on both parts, and no vow could be any purer or holier than this one. Evgenia's chaste charm sanctified Charles's love.)[66]

Comparing Balzac's and Dostoevsky's versions of this scene, one can see the greater emphasis that Dostoevsky places on Evgenia's connection to God and the sanctity of her love. In the concluding sentence, he uses a vocabulary that directly references church rhetoric: *promesse pure* becomes a "pure and holy vow" in Dostoevsky, *candeur* is replaces with "chaste charm." Dostoevsky also decides to omit Balzac's modifier *momentanément* because he sees it more fitting for the story if the virtue of Evgenia sanctified Charles's love not for a moment but forever. Eugénie's reaction to Charles's kiss, "ce n'est pas bien, dit-elle d'un accent peu grandeur," Dostoevsky changes to "Cousin, cousin!—she whispered in a tone of reproach." This substitution allows for a different interpretation of

---

65 Dostoevskii, *Evgeniia Grande*, 151.
66 Translation mine.

this important scene. In Balzac's original Eugénie is not really displeased with Charles's behavior and Balzac conveys it to the reader using a litote (*un accent peu grondeur*), but in Dostoevsky's version Evgenia is actually reproaching Charles. Dostoevsky did not see any need to allude to his character's conflicting feelings towards the sensual side of love. In his translation, Evgenia stays chaste throughout the novel as the symbolic embodiment of an angel on earth, despite the fact that Charles kissed her breast. Dostoevsky chose to downplay this moment by having Evgenia reproach Charles for his audacity.

In Dostoevsky's aesthetics, as in Balzac's view, happy love makes the woman beautiful, and when love leaves, her beauty vanishes. This idea is illustrated in the concluding pages of *Eugénie Grandet* where Balzac gives a detailed description of a mature Eugénie in her forties. Dostoevsky shares Balzac's notion of the fleeting nature of female beauty corresponding to the brevity of happiness in love. He later makes a strong point of beauty's transient character through Versilov's comments about the changed appearance of Sophia. Looking at the photograph, Versilov continues to talk to his adolescent son Arkady about a very brief moment when Sophia was as beautiful as she was captured in that portrait. He says that he cannot even imagine her with a young and happy face:

> Русские женщины дурнеют быстро, красота их только мелькнет, и, право, это не от одних только этнографических особенностей типа, а и оттого еще, что они умеют любить беззаветно. Русская женщина все разом отдает, коли полюбит,—и мгновение, и судьбу, и настоящее, и будущее: экономничать не умеют, про запас не прячут, и красота их быстро уходит в того, кого любят.[67]

> (Russian women lose their beauty quickly, their beauty only appears for a moment, and really, it's not just because of the particular ethnographical features of their type but also because they know how to love selflessly. A Russian woman gives all at once, if she loves—a moment, her destiny, and the present and the future: they do not know how to spare, they do not hide [keep] anything in reserve, and their beauty quickly goes to the one they love.)[68]

Here, Dostoevsky expresses his own thoughts on the ephemeral nature of woman's beauty and her generosity in love, her willingness to give all of

---

67 Dostoevskii, *Sobranie sochinenii v 15 tomakh*, 10:271.
68 Translation mine.

herself to her lover without holding anything back. This all-encompassing magnanimity, with constant readiness for self-sacrifice, is one of the important themes in many of Dostoevsky's novels.

When the relationship between Versilov and Sonya begins, it is described in very similar terms to Eugénie's first encounter with Charles. Eugénie considers herself too plain to be even noticed by Charles ("Je ne suis pas assez belle pour lui")[69] and Dostoevsky in his translation intensifies that feeling of inferiority to the object of desire by changing it to: "Я дурна, он и не заметит меня"[70] (I am ugly, he would not even notice me). Similarly to Eugénie, Dostoevsky's Sonya feels not worthy of Versilov. When Versilov talks about their relationship to Arkady, he recalls:

> Пуще всего меня мучило воспоминание о ее вечной приниженности передо мной и о том, что она вечно считала себя безмерно ниже меня во всех отношениях—вообрази себе—даже в физическом. Она стыдилась и вспыхивала, когда я иногда смотрел на ее руки и пальцы, которые у ней совсем не аристократические. Да и не пальцев одних, она всего стыдилась в себе, несмотря на то, что я любил ее красоту.[71]

> (Most of all I was tormented by the memory of her eternal humility in front of me, and that she always considered herself infinitely beneath me in every way—imagine—even physically. She was ashamed and flushed when I sometimes looked at her hands and fingers, which are not aristocratic at all. And not just fingers, she was ashamed of everything in herself, despite the fact that I loved her beauty.)[72]

In his novels, Dostoevsky equates humility and self-effacement in love with the sincerity of feeling and readiness for self-sacrifice that he first admired while reading and translating Balzac's masterpiece.

For Dostoevsky, though, the lasting attraction of Evgenia's character is not only her humility and ability to love deeply and selflessly but also her inner strength that she demonstrates in her confrontation with her father. At the turning point of the novel, when Grandet demands to know what she did with her gold, she simply says that this is her secret, just like her father who has his own secrets. All she says is that she used her money for

---

69 Balzac, *Eugénie Grandet*, 130.
70 Dostoevskii, *Evgeniia Grande*, 68.
71 Dostoevskii, *Sobranie sochinenii v 15 tomakh*, 10:286.
72 Translation mine.

a good cause. Grandet is completely surprised at the unexpected behavior of his always obedient daughter, and he begins to curse her and yell at her. Eugénie remains motionless and silent: "Il regarda sa fille, elle était toujours muette and froide.—Elle ne bougera pas, elle ne sourcillera pas, elle est plus Grandet, fistre,[73] que je ne suis Grandet"[74] (He looked at his daughter, who remained cold and silent. She won't budge, she won't flinch, she is more of a Grandet than I am!).[75] The unexpected resistance of Eugénie who always used to obey her father provokes Grandet to lock her in her room and only give her bread and water until she tells him what happened to her money. She accepts her father's will, and her confinement lasts for many months, but she does not complain and her reserve is unchanged.

Dostoevsky's ideal women share this combination of meekness and firmness in the face of circumstances that Eugénie demonstrated in that climactic moment of the novel. This is how Versilov talks to Arkady about Sonya:

> Смирение, безответность, приниженность и в то же время твердость, сила, настоящая сила—вот характер твоей матери. Заметь, что это лучшая из всех женщин, каких я встречал на свете. А что в ней сила есть—это я засвидетельствую; видал же я, как эта сила ее питала. Там, где касается, я не скажу убеждений—правильных убеждений тут быть не может, но того, что считается у них убеждением, стало быть, по-ихнему и святым, там просто хоть на муки.[76]

> (Meekness, unassertiveness, humility and at the same time, the firmness, strength, real strength—that's the nature of your mother. Note that she is the best of all women that I have seen in the world. And that she has strength—I will testify to that; I saw how that strength nourished her. As far as, I would not say beliefs—true beliefs can not exist here,—but what is considered by them a belief, therefore, in their language, it is sacred, they will go through torture for it.)[77]

---

73 In the quoted English translation this word is omitted, a Provençal dictionary gives the following definition: "fistre—interj., certe, peste, diantre" (Étienne Garcin, ed., *Nouveau dictionnaire provençal-français* [Draguignan, France: Chez Fabre, 1841], vol. 1, 391).

74 Balzac, *Eugénie Grandet*, 297.

75 Balzac, *Père Goriot, and Eugénie Grandet*, 446.

76 Dostoevskii, *Sobranie sochinenii v 15 tomakh*, 9:343.

77 Translation mine.

Versilov admires in Sophia the same readiness to accept suffering for her beliefs that Dostoevsky saw first in Eugénie's character. For Eugénie, it is her all-encompassing love for Charles that allows her stoically bear her father's anger, the illness and death of her mother, and several years of silence before her father's death. For Dostoevsky's ideal woman, love is also a sustaining force that helps her endure pain and suffering without complaint and without doubting divine providence.

Dashing Versilov with his latest Parisian fashion suddenly appears in the humble world of poor Sophia, and she is immediately captivated by his foreignness and brilliance, just as Balzac's Eugénie is enchanted by her Parisian cousin Charles. When Eugénie first sees Charles, she is completely mesmerized by his metropolitan aura and stylish appearance. The contrast between true Parisian chic, viewed at the time of Balzac's writing as the epitome of style, and the drab provincial background of Saumur and its inhabitants is so stark that Charles's arrival is compared to the sudden appearance of a seraph, precisely because it is so out of the ordinary in Eugénie's world:

> Eugénie, à qui le type d'une perfection semblable, soit dans la mise, soit dans la personne, était entièrement inconnu, crut voir en son cousin un créature descendue de quelque région séraphique. Elle respirait avec délices les parfums exhalés par cette chevelure si brillante, si gracieusement bouclée; elle aurait voulu pouvoir toucher la peau blanche de ses jolis gants de daim; elle enviait les petites mains de Charles, son teint, la fraîcheur et la délicatesse de ses traits.[78]

> (Eugénie, to whom such perfection either in dress or person was entirely unknown, saw in her cousin a creature descended from some heavenly region. She inhaled with delight the fragrance given off by that glossy hair so gracefully curled. She would have liked to touch the satiny white kid of those exquisite gloves; she envied Charles his small hands, his complexion, the freshness and delicacy of his features.)[79]

Balzac's description of Charles's first appearance in the novel includes several elements usually associated with feminine gender: fragrance, small hands, "gracefully curled hair," delicacy of complexion and facial features. By contrast, Eugénie's physical appearance has some masculine traits: she

---

78 Balzac, *Eugénie Grandet*, 93.
79 Balzac, *Père Goriot, and Eugénie Grandet*, 330.

is described as *grande et forte* ("tall" or "heavy-set" and "strong"). This curious interchange of traditional gender attributes is not as important for Dostoevsky, who instead focuses his attention on the stark contrast between the luxury of urban aristocratic lifestyle embodied by Charles and the frugal and austere life in the country, embodied by Grandet and his circle. This will become a recurrent theme in Dostoevsky's own writing later on.

The same striking contrast between the lifestyle of the capital and gray humdrum life of the provinces, the capital's exorbitant display of wealth and brilliance, and outward sophistication in dress and manners is present in Dostoevsky's novel at the starting point of the relationship between Versilov and Sophia. Their first encounter is a parallel of Evgenia's first meeting with Charles. Versilov's excellent French, hairstyle, and manners have a similar spellbinding effect on Sophia. The description in the *Raw Youth* is very brief; Dostoevsky only focuses on a few salient details describing Versilov (his hairstyle, French accent, and his music):

> Может быть, она полюбила до смерти . . . фасон его платья, парижский пробор волос, его французский выговор, именно французский, в котором она не понимала ни звука, тот романс, который он спел за фортепиано, полюбила нечто никогда не виданное и не слыханное (а он был очень красив собою), и уж заодно полюбила, прямо до изнеможения, всего его, с фасонами и романсами.[80]

> (Maybe she fell in love deeply . . . with a style of his dress, his Parisian hairstyle parted in the middle, his French way of speaking, it was precisely French, of which she did not understand a sound, with the song that he sang at the piano, she fell in love with something never seen or heard before [and he was very handsome], and even at the same time fell in love with, almost unbearably, all of him, with his style and romances.)[81]

Both novels share a similar starting point—an unhappy love relationship between a dashing dandy and a simple provincial girl, found in many romantic novels of the period. However, the development of the story is very different in Dostoevsky's novel because of his treatment of Versilov's character. Even though Versilov in the beginning appears as a dandy and a rogue, over the course of the novel his character undergoes a deep spiritual

---

80 Dostoevskii, *Sobranie sochinenii v 15 tomakh*, 9:226.
81 Translation mine.

transformation, he attains a better understanding of himself, he promises to marry Sophia, and at the end he is portrayed living with her by his side.

It is important to point out that in his translation of Balzac, in the final pages of the novel, Dostoevsky refers to Evgenia as an angel, while this comparison is missing in Balzac's text in that specific part. Balzac' s original contains the following: "Dieu jeta donc des masses d'or à sa prisonnière pour qui l'or était indifférent, qui aspirait au ciel; qui vivait, pieuse et bonne, en saintes pensées; qui secourait incessamment les malheureux, en secret"[82] (God flung masses of gold to his prisoner who was indifferent to gold and who yearned for heaven, who lived, pious and good, in holy thoughts, who constantly gave aid in secret to those in distress).[83] In Dostoevsky's translation, this sentence acquired a much more pronounced religious coloring: "Бог пролил золото и блага земные перед бедным ангелом, которого Он послал на землю заслужить свою долю небесную" (God poured gold and earthly rewards in front of the poor angel whom he sent to earth to earn her place in heaven).[84]

Time and again, Dostoevsky returns to his image of an ideal woman— an angel sent to earth to save the wretched souls and to redeem the sins of others with her suffering. This image of a virtuous woman as an angel on earth who is tending to the wounds of the sick and saving the wretched found its incarnation in the finale of *The Raw Youth*: the loving and kind Sonya, whom Versilov called his angel before leaving her, [85] nurses him back to health after his attempted suicide. She is able to heal his spiritual wounds after his infatuation with Yekaterina Nikolaevna, thus fulfilling her angelic role in his fate and his earlier prophecy. In the final pages of the novel, the sick Versilov is recovering at Sonya's home and treats her with new tenderness:

> Рана его оказалась не смертельною и зажила, но пролежал он довольно долго—у мамы, разумеется. Теперь, когда я пишу эти строки,—на дворе весна, половина мая, день прелестный, и у нас отворены окна. Мама сидит около него; он гладит рукой ее щеки и волосы и с умилением

---

82 Balzac, *Eugénie Grandet*, 379.

83 Balzac, *Père Goriot, and Eugénie Grandet*, 495.

84 Translation mine.

85 "А все-таки к тебе вернусь, к последнему ангелу!" (I will still return to you, my last angel!), Dostoevskii, *Sobranie sochinenii v 15 tomakh*, 10:321.

засматривает ей в глаза. О, это только половина прежнего Версилова; от мамы он уж не отходит и уж никогда не отойдет более.[86]

(His wound was not fatal and healed, but he spent a long time in bed—at my mother's place, of course. Now, as I write these lines—outside it is spring, the middle of May, the day is lovely and we opened the windows. Mama is sitting beside him; he strokes her cheeks and hair with his hand and tenderly looks into her eyes. Oh, and that's only half of the old Versilov; he will not step away from Mama and certainly will never leave her again.)

Not only does Versilov acquire humility and tenderness towards Sophia, he also finally accepts her religious faith. For any of Dostoevsky's characters, it constitutes a crucial step towards spiritual enlightenment and redemption. One should also note that this novel ends with a reversal of fortune, a device frequently found in Balzac's novels and beloved by Dostoevsky: the rich lose their fortune and shed their pride (Versilov); they become humble and rely on the kindness and magnanimity of those whom they wronged in the past (Sophia).

The Portrayal of Sonya in Crime and Punishment (1866)

The theme of meek suffering and noble self-sacrifice in Dostoevsky's poetics finds its ultimate incarnation many years later in another Sonya, a character in what is arguably the best-known novel by Dostoevsky—*Crime and Punishment*. In this novel, in accordance with Dostoevsky's system of moral values, Sonya is a fallen woman, but she is deeply virtuous and pure; she makes the radical choice to work in prostitution in order to save her stepmother Katerina Ivanovna and her young siblings from starvation. This great sacrifice is driven by her deep love for the children of Katerina Ivanovna and her boundless compassion for the tragic situation of her family. For Dostoevsky, Sonya's character is the embodiment of the Christian virtues of brotherly love, humility, and self-sacrifice. It is Sonya who, with her unwavering religious faith, saves Raskolnikov from the depths of spiritual despair after he commits two murders. After his trial, Sonya follows him to the hard labor camps in Siberia, where she becomes a guardian angel for Raskolnikov and for the other prisoners.

---

86 Ibid., 368.

When Raskolnikov first sees Sonya, he does not find her face pretty, but her eyes, similarly to those of Balzac's Eugénie, are her best feature and they immediately draw his attention:

> Это было худенькое, совсем худенькое и бледное личико, довольно неправильное, какое-то востренькое, с востреньким маленьким носом и подбородком. Ее даже нельзя было назвать и хорошенькою, но зато голубые глаза ее были такие ясные, и, когда оживлялись они, выражение лица ее становилось такое доброе и простодушное, что невольно привлекало к ней.[87]

> (She had a thin little face, quite thin and pale, and rather irregular, somehow sharp, with a sharp little nose and chin. She could not even have been called pretty, but her blue eyes were so clear, and when they were animated, the expression of her face became so kind and simple-hearted, that one involuntarily felt drawn to her.)[88]

In this first portrayal of Sonya through Raskolnikov's eyes, we notice the repeated elements of clarity (ясность) and kindness (доброта) that Dostoevsky frequently uses in the descriptions of his best female characters. One remembers that in Balzac's novel, Eugénie's eyes are also the most remarkable feature of her face, and they evoke the eyes of Raphael's Madonna, in which one can glimpse "something of the divine." Describing Sonya's physical appearance, the narrator says directly that she is not conventionally pretty, but the reader sees the same recurring element of Dostoevsky's writing—there is a true inner beauty hidden from view and only shining through the eyes, since the eyes are traditionally viewed as a "mirror of the soul."[89]

---

87 Dostoevskii, *Sobranie sochinenii v 15 tomakh*, 5:230.

88 Dostoevsky, *Crime and Punishment*, 238.

89 Similarly, Tolstoy in *War and Peace*, in his portrayal of Princess Marya emphasizes her marvelous eyes though which her inner beauty shines even though her face is plain: "глаза княжны, большие, глубокие и лучистые (как будто лучи теплого света иногда снопами выходили из них), были так хороши, что очень часто, несмотря на некрасивость всего лица, глаза эти делались привлекательнее красоты" (Lev Tolstoy, *Voina i Mir*, vol. 1 [Moscow and Leningrad, Russia: Izdatel'stvo khudozhestvennoi literatury, 1960], 97). In English translation, "the Princess's eyes, large, deep and luminous (at times rays of warm light seemed to radiate from them), were really so beautiful that very often, in spite of the plainness of her face, they gave her an allure greater than beauty" (Leo Tolstoy, *War and Peace*, trans. Ann Dunningan [New York: Penguin Books, 1968], 127).

In the novel's epilogue, Sonya's angelic kindness and compassion achieve their pinnacle when she follows Raskolnikov to Siberia. She is portrayed as an angel for prisoners. Raskolnikov at first is perplexed why Sonya is so loved by the convicts:

> Неразрешим был для него еще один вопрос: почему все они так полюбили Соню? Она у них не заискивала; встречали они ее редко, иногда только на работах, когда она приходила на одну минутку, чтобы повидать его. А между тем все уже знали ее, знали и то, что она *за ним* последовала, знали, как она живет, где живет. Денег она им не давала, особенных услуг не оказывала. Раз только, на Рождестве, принесла она на весь острог подаяние: пирогов и калачей. Но мало-помалу между ними и Соней завязались некоторые более близкие отношения: она писала им письма к их родным и отправляла их на почту. Их родственники и родственницы, приезжавшие в город, оставляли, по указанию их, в руках Сони вещи для них и даже деньги. . . . И когда она являлась на работах, приходя к Раскольникову, или встречалась с партией арестантов, идущих на работы,—все снимали шапки, все кланялись: "Матушка, Софья Семеновна, мать ты наша, нежная, болезная!"—говорили эти грубые, клейменые каторжные этому маленькому и худенькому созданию.[90]

(Still another question remained insoluble for him: why had they all come to love Sonya so much? She had not tried to win them over, they met her only rarely, and work now and then, when she would come for a moment to see him. And yet they all knew her, knew also that she had followed *after him*, knew how she lived and where she lived. She had never given them money or done them any special favors. Only once, at Christmas, she brought alms for the whole prison: pies and kalatchi. But, little by little, certain closer relations sprang up between them and Sonya. She wrote letters for them to their families, and posted them. When their male or female relatives came to town, they would instruct them to leave things and even money for them in Sonya's hands. . . . And when she came to see Raskolnikov at work, or met a party of convicts on the way to work, they would all take their hats off, they would all bow to her: "Dear mother, Sofya Semyonovna, our tender, fond

---

90 Dostoevskii, *Sobranie sochinenii v 15 tomakh*, 5:529.

dear mother!"—so the coarse, branded convicts would say to this small and frail being.)[91]

One can say that Sonya's role as a guardian angel on earth in the epilogue is similar to Eugénie's charitable deeds in the epilogue of Balzac's novel. But Balzac mentions only in passing that the mature Eugénie has a habit of helping those in need and healing the wounds of the suffering. In contrast, Dostoevsky greatly amplifies the natural goodness and kindliness of his selfless character in *Crime and Punishment*. Sonya is viewed by the most miserable stratum of the population—the convicts at hard labor—as their angel. They love and respect her and even seek medical help from her: "К ней даже ходили лечиться."[92]

The motif of great inner strength behind a fragile exterior was already seen in the portrait of the main female character in *The Meek One* and other works of Dostoevsky discussed above. When Balzac's Eugénie is forced to go through the confrontation with her father, she is still an innocent young girl, but she is able to find the source of her resolve to resist her father in her love for Charles. For Balzac's poetic world, a woman's defining moment is her ability to love, as shown not only in *Eugénie Grandet* but in many of his other novels—*Le Père Goriot*, *Les Illusions perdues*, *Splendeurs et misères des courtisanes*, *Lys dans la vallée*, *La Femme abandonnée*, and *La Duchesse de Langeais,* among others. For Dostoevsky, it is not a woman's love for a man but love for Christ and deep religious faith that is the cornerstone of human existence. He takes the theme of meek resistance, which he first discovered in Evgenia and develops it in the context of his philosophical beliefs.

Similarly to Eugénie/Evgenia, Dostoevsky's ideal women are usually young and innocent; they manifest great firmness in the face of adversity, as Sonya does on the streets of Saint Petersburg, or in hard labor camps; and they find the source of their spiritual strength not in love but in their religious faith. When Raskolnikov first visits Sonya, he is stunned by the destitute atmosphere of her surroundings and her tragic personal situation from which he sees no escape. He begins to search for a reason that prevents her from committing suicide or going mad or "throwing herself into debauchery," and is surprised to discover that her ability to go on with the horror of her daily life, safeguard the purity of her soul, and not fall into despair is rooted in her religion.

---

91 Dostoevsky, *Crime and Punishment*, 546.
92 Dostoevskii, *Sobranie sochinenii v 15 tomakh*, 5:529.

Он начал пристальнее всматриваться в нее.

—Так ты очень молишься Богу-то, Соня?—спросил он ее.

Соня молчала, он стоял подле нее и ждал ответа.

—Что ж бы я без Бога-то была?—быстро, энергически прошептала она, мельком вскинув на него вдруг засверкавшими глазами, и крепко стиснула рукой его руку.[93]

(He began studying her with great attention.

"So you pray very much to God, Sonya?" he asked her.

Sonya was silent; he stood beside her, waiting for an answer.

"And what would I be without God?" she whispered quickly, energetically, glancing at him fleetingly with suddenly flashing eyes, and she pressed his hand firmly with her own.")[94]

This conversation highlights a principle that is key to Dostoevsky's writings: that Sonya's moral strength is nurtured by her passionate faith in God. Religious faith is central to Dostoevsky's poetics and his personal system of values. Dostoevsky was an ardent believer in the teachings of Christianity; he felt that love for Christ is what would keep a person on a righteous path. On the contrary, lack of religious faith leads a person to err in judgment and actions. This theme was fully developed in *The Brothers Karamazov*, but a precursor can be seen in *Crime and Punishment* and even earlier, in 1854, in Dostoevsky's letter to Nadezhda Fonvizina. In that letter, Dostoevsky makes a striking admission that if he was to choose between Christ and truth, he would remain with Christ: "If someone were to prove me that Christ is outside the truth, and it were indeed so, I would rather remain with Christ than with the truth"[95] ("если б кто мне доказал, что Христос вне истины, и *действительно* было бы, что истина вне Христа, то мне лучше хотелось бы оставаться со Христом, нежели с истиной").[96] This seemingly paradoxical statement illustrates the specificity of Dostoevsky's own interpretation of Christianity. He was far more interested in the figure of Christ as a personal embodiment of suffering, selfless love, and sacrifice, than in the abstract scholastic dogmas of the Orthodox tradition.

Balzac's view on religion is very different from Dostoevsky's. At the center of Balzac's religious beliefs is a more abstract concept of divine

---

93   Ibid., 5:313.

94   Dostoevsky, *Crime and Punishment*, 323.

95   Translation mine.

96   Dostoevskii, *Sobranie sochinenii v 15 tomakh*, 15:96.

providence, whose invisible hand is sometimes responsible for plot resolution in his novels. However, as with Dostoevsky, Balzac's positive characters are striving to do what is right in the eyes of God and Christian morality. In *Eugénie Grandet*, Eugénie and her pious mother regularly pray to God, and their prayers help them sustain their moral strength in the face of cruel treatment from Grandet. For Eugénie, prayers help to ease the pain of her solitude and separation from Charles, and later support her through the illness and death of her mother. Not surprisingly, Old Grandet is not religious and mocks the devotion of his wife and daughter.

The powerful image of Balzac's Eugénie had a profound influence on young Dostoevsky and found its many reincarnations in his later works, as has been demonstrated in this chapter. In his free translation of Balzac's novel, Dostoevsky consciously focused on the features of the central character that he found especially resonant when considering his own moral values: her ability to love deeply and passionately, her inner strength, and her great gifts of endless compassion and self-sacrifice. Consequently, in Dostoevsky's translation the character of Evgenia acquired a much stronger religious coloring and deeper connection to heaven, chastity, and virtue. Dostoevsky even made conscious changes, omissions, and additions to the text in his translations in order to emphasize these moral traits, and which later reappeared in the images of ideal female characters in his other works.

Chapter Two

The Material World in Balzac's *Eugénie Grandet* and in Dostoevsky's Texts

Balzac was intensely interested in providing plentiful and specific details about his characters' surroundings and physical spaces in his novels, striving to recreate for his readers as fully as possible the material world of Paris or the French provinces. He densely populated *La Comédie humaine* with precise description of architecture, upholstery fabrics, furniture, fashionable clothing, accessories, and many more attributes of French daily life. In his translation of *Eugénie Grandet*, the young Dostoevsky wanted to make Balzac's richly depicted and concrete French world accessible to average Russian readers, many of whom had never been abroad and could not fully understand the specific details of Balzac's settings for his novels. Throughout his translation, the young Dostoevsky made a series of conscious choices to eliminate some obscure names of textiles, descriptions of wine-making terms and barrel-making techniques, as well as other words and concepts that were difficult to understand for the Russian readers without extensive commentary and explanatory notes. He chose instead to amplify and bring into focus the passages that he found the most appealing as a reader and a writer—those describing the emotional tension and psychological conflict in the novel. As a result of this creative approach, in some places Balzac's original was shortened; in others, the translation became longer. This chapter aims to trace the connections between Dostoevsky's use of Balzac's technique of creating the material world in his novels and its reflection in Dostoevsky's later works.

Houses and Rooms in *Eugénie Grandet* and Dostoevsky's Works

Analyzing the role of description in Balzac's works, researchers and biographers[1] agree that a detailed and precise description of the characters' physical environment is very important for Balzac's technique as a writer. In all of *La Comédie humaine* there is a strong connection between the personality of the character (*l'esprit*) and the physical space (*milieu*) that the character occupies. This Balzacian technique of reflecting the inner world of the character in its immediate environment stems from the tradition of *la théorie du milieu*, a French philosophical theory that took its origins in the end of the eighteenth century and connected a person's spirit to his or her surroundings. Through detailed descriptions of personal space, Balzac reveals to the reader the inner psychology, temperament, and general personality of his characters.

For example, in *Le Père Goriot* a long description of Rastignac's shabby and old boarding house is provided first; its proprietor, Madame Vauquer, is then described. A strong connection between her unkempt and somewhat grotesque appearance and her bleak, worn- out boardinghouse, decorated in hideously bad taste, is openly stated in the text: "toute sa personne explique la pension, comme la pension implique sa personne"[2] (Her whole person gives a clue[3] to the boardinghouse; just as the boarding house implies such a mistress as Madame Vauquer).[4] On the opposite end of the spectrum, the refined and luxurious rooms of Madame de Beauséant are in perfect harmony with her character's beauty, sensitivity, and intelligence.

This symbolic role of description became the trademark not only of Balzac but also of many realist authors of the nineteenth century, such as Zola, Stendhal, and Flaubert. For Dostoevsky, a strong connection between the characters and their physical space also became a very important device, which he employed repeatedly in describing physical spaces and rooms in all of his great novels. Most probably, young Dostoevsky's close interaction

---

1   See Henry James, "The Lesson of Balzac. Two Lectures," *Atlantic Monthly*, August 1905, 166–180; Donald Fanger, *Dostoevsky and Romantic Realism* (Cambridge: Harvard University Press, 1965); Judith Wechsler, *A Human Comedy: Physiognomy and Caricature in Nineteenth-Century Paris* (Chicago: University of Chicago Press, 1982).
2   Honoré De Balzac, *La Comédie humaine: Études de moeurs: Scènes de la vie privée*, ed. Marcel Bouteron, vol. 2 (Paris: Gallimard, 1948), 852.
3   A more literal translation is "explains the boarding house."
4   Balzac, *Père Goriot, and Eugénie Grandet*, 9.

with Balzac's text had a profound impact on the later use of the descriptions of physical spaces in his own works.

At the same time, there are differences in Balzac and Dostoevsky's approaches to describing physical space that become evident if one compares closely the opening of the French original of *Eugénie Grandet* and Dostoevsky's translation of the same passage. In the first paragraph, Balzac concentrates the readers' attention on the setting by providing a metaphorically rich, poetically evocative description of the house of Grandet.

> Il se trouve dans certaines provinces des maisons dont la vue inspire une mélancolie égale à celle que provoquent les cloîtres les plus sombres, les landes les plus ternes ou les ruines les plus tristes. Peut-être y a-t-il à la fois dans ces maisons et le silence du cloître et l'aridité des landes et les ossements des ruines. La vie et le mouvement y sont si tranquilles qu'un étranger les croirait inhabitées, s'il ne rencontrait tout à coup le regard pâle et froid d'une personne immobile dont la figure à demi monastique dépasse l'appui de la croisée, au bruit d'un pas inconnu. Ces principes de mélancolie existent dans la physionomie d'un logis situé à Saumur, au bout de la rue montueuse qui mène au château, par le haut de la ville.[5]

> (In certain provincial towns there are houses that create a feeling of melancholy equal to that aroused by the gloomiest cloisters, the bleakest moorland, or the most mournful ruins. Perhaps they combine the stillness of the cloister, the barrenness of the moors, and the desiccation of the ruins. The life within them moves so slowly that a stranger would suppose them uninhabited were he not suddenly to encounter the pale, cold gaze of a motionless figure, whose half-monastic face appears above the window ledge at the sound of an unfamiliar footstep. These melancholy elements are present in the physiognomy of a dwelling in Saumur, at the end of a steep street leading to the castle by way of the upper town.)[6]

Balzac's creative method was to present to the readers the whole history of a building hiding behind its facade. Stefan Zweig in his comparative study *Balzac, Dickens, Dostoevsky: Master Builders of the Spirit* noted Balzac's remarkable ability of observation saying that Balzac, as

---

5   Balzac, *Eugénie Grandet*, 23.
6   Idem, *Père Goriot, and Eugénie Grandet*, 293.

a master flâneur, . . . knew by the mere look of a house when it had been built, by whom and for whom; he deciphered the coat-of-arms over the door, and had thoughts of the appropriate epoch called by the architecture; he could make a shrewd guess at the rent, peopled every story with occupants, placed furniture in the rooms, and tenanted them with happy folk or unhappy; from floor to floor, he traced the network of destiny that enmeshed the whole building and its inhabitants.[7]

Balzac's descriptions are always rich in specific details and suggestive of a certain mood, yet at the same time rather static, created like a stage on which the plot can develop. In his translation, Dostoevsky describes Grandet's house in a more active way than Balzac by adding many more verbs, especially those that denote movement:

Иногда в провинции встречаешь жилища, с виду мрачные и унылые, как древние монастыри, как дикие грустные развалины, как сухие, бесплодные, обнаженные степи; заглянув под крыши этих жилищ, и в самом деле часто найдешь жизнь вялую, скучную, напоминающую своим однообразием и тишину монастырскую, и скуку обнаженных, диких степей, и прах развалин. Право, проходя возле дверей такого дома, невольно сочтёшь его необитаемым; но скоро, однако ж, разуверишься: подождав немного, непременно увидишь сухую, мрачную фигуру хозяина, привлечённого к окну шумом шагов на улице. Такой мрачный вид уныния, казалось, был отличительным признаком одного дома в городе Сомюре.

(Sometimes in the provinces you meet a house that is gloomy and sad in appearance, like the ancient monasteries, like wild sad ruins, like dry, barren, bare steppes; looking under the roofs of these houses, in fact one often finds life there sluggish, boring, and resembling in its monotony the silence of the monastery, the boredom of naked, wild steppes, and the dust of debris. Indeed, passing by the door of such a house, you could consider it uninhabited; soon, however, you would be convinced otherwise: after a short wait you would surely see the thin, somber figure of the owner, attracted to the window by the noise of steps outside. Such a somber look of gloom seemed to be the distinguishing mark of a house in the city of Saumur.)

---

7   Stefan Zweig, *Balzac, Dickens, Dostoevsky: Master Builders of the Spirit* (Somerset, NJ: Transaction, 2010), 39.

Dostoevsky structures the opening sentence differently by saying not that the look of these houses inspired melancholy, but that the dwellings appeared somber and melancholy as ancient convents ("жилища с виду мрачные и унылые, как древние монастыри"). Also, while Balzac uses the superlative degree of adjectives, Dostoevsky substitutes a string of adjectives. For example, *les cloîtres les plus sombres* (the darkest convents) become simply *древние монастыри* (ancient monasteries), *les ruines les plus tristes* (the saddest ruins) are changed to *дикие грустные развалины* (savage, sad ruins), and *les landes les plus ternes* (the dull lands) become *сухие, бесплодные, обнаженные степи* (arid, barren, naked steppes). Dostoevsky uses this method of adding adjectives repeatedly throughout the novel. Ultimately, the Russian version of the text grew in length and the Russian translation lost the three-part rhythm of Balzac's sentences. Balzac tends to present triads of adjectives and nouns in his descriptions, for example, *les cloîtres les plus sombres, les landes les plus ternes ou les ruines les plus tristes*. This sentence structure creates musicality and a certain, poetic rhythm. The Russian translation breaks this structure.

Another noticeable departure from the original is that Dostoevsky inserts the second-person singular verb forms as if adding an observer who addresses an imaginary reader right away in an informal, conversational manner: *встречаешь жилища* (you encounter the dwellings), *заглянув— найдёшь* (having looked inside, you will find), *проходя—сочтёшь его необитаемым* (passing by, you will think it uninhabited), *но скоро разуверишься* (but soon you will be convinced otherwise), *подождав, увидишь* (having waited, you will see). In this paragraph Dostoevsky uses eight verbs and gerunds in the second-person singular. This makes Dostoevsky's opening considerably more dynamic and action-driven than Balzac's. Later, in his own novels and short stories, the mature Dostoevsky would have his narrator openly engage the readers by addressing them directly in the foreword or in the main part of the text.

Looking further at the two excerpts, one notices that the phrase *les principes de mélancolie* (principles of melancholy) is replaced with *мрачный вид уныния* (somber look of melancholy). The words *la physionomie d'un logis* (physiognomy of a building) is absent completely in Dostoevsky's translation, but the word *физиономия* (physiognomy) would reappear later in Dostoevsky's description of Rogozhin's house in *The Idiot*, discussed later in this chapter.

In the opening passages of the novel Balzac emphasizes the gloom, decay, and darkness of Grandet's house, setting the scene for the tragic events that unfold later in the novel:

> La maison pleine de mélancolie où se sont accomplis les événements de cette histoire était précisément un de ces logis, restes vénérables d'un siècle où les choses et les hommes avaient ce caractère de simplicité que les moeurs françaises perdent de jour en jour.
>
> Après avoir suivi les détours de ce chemin pittoresque dont les moindres accidents réveillent des souvenirs et dont l'effet général tend à plonger dans une sorte de rêverie machinale, vous apercevez un renfoncement assez sombre, au centre duquel est cachée la porte de la maison à monsieur Grandet.
>
> Mais il est impossible de comprendre la valeur de cette expression provinciale sans donner la biographie de monsieur Grandet.[8]
>
> (The gloom-filled house in which the events of this story took place was precisely one of these dwellings, venerable relics of a century in which men and things were characterized by a simplicity that French manners and customs are losing day by day. Follow the windings of this picturesque thoroughfare, whose slightest irregularities awaken memories and whose general effect tends to plunge you into a kind of automatic reverie, and you will come upon a rather dark recess, in the middle of which is hidden the door of Monsieur Grandet. It is impossible to understand the full force of this provincial locution—the house of Monsieur Grandet[9]—without giving the biography of Grandet himself.)[10]

Dostoevsky brings several changes to the text, again making it more dynamic. This time, he inserts a fictional first-person narrator into the description, using the pronoun *мы* (we), which joins "you, the readers" with "I, the narrator." Moreover, in Balzac's original one notices the colloquial usage of preposition *à* denoting possession *la maison à monsieur Grandet*. This is typical of regional French, as opposed to the normative usage *la maison de monsieur Grandet*. In Russian it is not possible to convey the

---

8 Balzac, *Eugénie Grandet*, 6.
9 Unfortunately, in English it is not possible to replicate the Provençal dialect expression *maison à Monsieur Grandet* vs. the normative *maison de Monsieur Grandet*.
10 Balzac, *Père Goriot, and Eugénie Grandet*, 296.

difference between the two constructions; both constructions can only be translated, using the genitive case for possession, as *дом господина Гранде* (the house of Monsieur Grandet). Dostoevsky completely omits Balzac's reference to the local dialect.

The dialectal usage, along with other precise details, creates a particular atmosphere of the novel's main setting before any of the characters appear. In the beginning of the novel, Balzac strives to convey to his readers the sense of a melancholy "facial expression" of the houses, and in the last sentence he ties it explicitly to the life story of his main character: "Il est impossible de comprendre la valeur de cette expression provinciale sans donner la biographie de monsieur Grandet" (It is impossible to understand the value of this provincial expression without giving the biography of Monsieur Grandet).[11] Thus, from the extensive description of the setting the reader is transported into the plot. Twelve pages later, having introduced Old Grandet, his family, and the story behind his fortune, Balzac deftly concludes by returning to his initial statement: "It est maintenent facile de comprendre toute la valeur de ce mot, la maison à monsieur Grandet, cette maison pale, froide, silencieuse, située en haut de la ville, et abritée par les ruines des remparts "[12] (It is easy now to understand the full force of the term 'the house of'[13] Monsieur Grandet,' that bleak, cold, silent house in the upper town under the shadow of the walls).[14]

Here is Dostoevsky's translation of this passage:

Дом, мрачный и угрюмый, куда сейчас перенесем мы читателей, был из числа этих древних зданий, остаток старых дел, памятник старого времени, времени простого и незатейливого, от которого давно уже мы отреклись и отступились. Пройдя с вами по дороге, так богатой воспоминаниями, навевающими и грусть, и думу о прошедшем, я укажу вам на это мрачное углубление, посреди которого притаились ворота дома господина Гранде. Но мы не поймем всего значения, всего смысла фразы: дом господина Гранде—нужно познакомиться сначала с самим господином Гранде.[15]

---

11 Translation mine.
12 Balzac, *Eugénie Grandet*, 18.
13 A more precise translation is "belonging to."
14 Balzac, *Père Goriot, and Eugénie Grandet*, 306.
15 Dostoevskii, *Evgeniia Grande*, 9.

(The house, dark and gloomy, to which now we will transport the readers, was one of those ancient buildings, remnants of old affairs, a monument to old time, simple and unpretentious time that we have long since renounced and given up. Having walked with you on a path so rich in memories, evoking sadness and thoughts about the past, I'll point out to you this dark recess, in the middle of which lurks the gate to Mr. Grandet's house. But we cannot comprehend the full significance, the whole meaning of the phrase "the house of Mr. Grandet." We must first meet Mr. Grandet himself.)

Compared to Balzac, Dostoevsky uses here, as in the opening passage, many more verbs (eight in total) that agree with the subject in the first-person plural pronoun "we." He also explicitly states, "we will transport the reader" to this house—a phrase not evident in Balzac's text. Whereas Balzac ends the description with *vous apercevez* (you notice), Dostoevsky makes it narrator-centered by saying, "I will point out to you" (*я укажу вам*). Dostoevsky also changes the subjectless construction of the last sentence, *il est impossible du comprendre*, into an active construction "we will not comprehend" (*но мы не поймем*). Using the pronoun *мы* (we), Dostoevsky joins the readers and the narrator in a single group, placing the reader right in the middle of the narrative. Thus, he makes the text more reader-oriented and directed to the imaginary audience. Here one sees the beginnings of the dialogical quality of the narrative that became a trademark of Dostoevsky's writing style in his later novels.

Dostoevsky also employed Balzac's technique of detailed description of a setting in his portrayal of Saint Petersburg (see *White Nights*, a novel that was published in 1848, shortly after his translation, or *Crime and Punishment*). His meticulous descriptions of the city and its houses not only created for the reader an impression of a physical setting of the plot but established a direct connection between that physical space and the characters' inner world. The city itself, moreover, became one of the characters in the story.

A salient example of a physical space reflecting the inner world of a character appears in *Crime and Punishment* (1866). Raskolnikov's mother and his sister visit him in his tiny room after he has committed the murder. His mother is struck not only by Raskolnilov's cold reaction to their visit but by the poverty and generally depressed atmosphere of his room:

Какая у тебя дурная квартира, Родя, точно гроб,—сказала вдруг Пульхерия Александровна, прерывая тягостное молчание,—я уверена, что ты наполовину от квартиры стал такой меланхолик.

—Квартира? . .—отвечал он рассеянно.—Да, квартира много способствовала . . . я об этом тоже думал. . . .[16]

("What an awful apartment you have, Rodya; like a coffin," Pulcheria Alexandrovna said suddenly breaking the heavy silence. "I'm sure that it's half on the account of this apartment that you've become so melancholic." "Apartment ? . ." he replied distractedly. "Yes, the apartment contributed a lot . . . I' ve thought about that myself. . . .")[17]

The descriptions of Raskolnikov's room confirm the explicit connection between the physical surroundings of a character and his or her psychological and emotional state, which was so important for Balzac and evident in his treatment of Old Grandet's house. Already in the opening paragraphs of *Crime and Punishment*, Raskolnikov's extremely small room—*kamorka*—is compared to a closet, evoking the sense of dark enclosed space and general discomfort. When later Raskolnikov's mother suddenly compares his room to a coffin, that comparison also evokes for the reader an extremely small, tight, and sinister place. Moreover, the coffin as a symbol connects Raskolnikov with death and alludes to the tragic events in his life.

Similarly, in *Eugénie Grandet*, in the first description of Old Grandet's bleak, gloomy house, Balzac concentrates the readers' attention on an entrance with a heavy old front door and a small iron grill opening, making an explicit comparison to a jail.

Les trous, inégaux et nombreux que les intempéries du climat y avaient bizarrrement pratiqués, donnaient au cintre et aux jambages de la baie l'apparence de pierres vermiculées de l'architecture française et quelque resemblance avec le porche d'un geôle. . . . La porte, en chêne massif, brune, desséchée, fendue de toutes parts, frêle en apparence, était solidement maintenue par le système de ses boulons qui figuraient des dessins symétriques. Une grille carrée, petite, mais à barreaux serrés et rouges de rouille, occupait le milieu de la porte bâtarde et servait, pour ainsi dire, de

---

16 Dostoevskii, *Sobranie sochinenii v 15 tomakh*, 5:224.
17 Dostoevsky, *Crime and Punishment*, 231.

motif à un marteau qui s'y rattachait par un anneau et frappait sur la tête grimaçaint d'un maître clou.[18]

(The many irregular cavities, oddly hollowed out by the inclemency of the weather, gave the arch and pillars of the bay a resemblance to the vermiculated stonework characteristic of French architecture and made it look something like the gateway of a jail. . . . The door of the archway was of solid oak, brown, dried up, cracked in all directions, and, though frail in appearance, was stoutly reinforced by a system of bolts arranged in symmetrical designs. A little square grating, its closely set bars red with rust, in the middle of the small door cut in the larger one, served, so to speak, as motif for a knocker, which was attached to it by a ring and which struck on the grimacing head of an enormous nail.)[19]

The imagery in this passage evokes not only decay, aging, and deterioration that come with the passage of time. There are also several elements that directly reference prison space: a massive oak door, heavily reinforced by many bolts; a heavy knocker; and a small rusty iron grate on the door to see who is coming. Later in the novel, the reader is reminded of that comparison as Old Grandet literally makes his daughter a prisoner in his house, forbidding her to leave the house when she disobeys him. Thus, the heavy massive door with a small iron grill can be viewed as a semiotic sign, as frequently occurs in Balzac's long descriptions with their meaningful details. In semiotics, any object can become a sign invested with special interpretive meaning that lies beyond its direct function. In this example, the massive lock on the door can be interpreted in the direct sense as protecting the house from the intruders, but from juxtaposing it to other visual details that Balzac chose to highlight in the description of the house, the reader can perceive that the lock stands for metaphorically barring Eugenie from leaving her domineering father.

Dostoevsky would remember these suggestive details: irregular shapes, thick walls, darkness, and numerous locked doors appear again in *Crime and Punishment* when he describes Sonya's room with its ugly disturbing irregular angles and low oppressive ceiling.

---

18 Balzac, *Eugénie Grandet*, 49.
19 Balzac, *Père Goriot, and Eugénie Grandet*, 307.

Это была большая комната, но чрезвычайно низкая, единственная отдававшаяся от Капернаумовых, запертая дверь к которым находилась в стене слева. На противоположной стороне, в стене справа, была еще другая дверь, всегда запертая наглухо. Там уже была другая, соседняя квартира, под другим нумером. Сонина комната походила как будто на сарай, имела вид весьма неправильного четыреугольника, и это придавало ей что-то уродливое. Стена с тремя окнами, выходившая на канаву, перерезывала комнату как-то вкось, отчего один угол, ужасно острый, убегал куда-то вглубь, так что его, при слабом освещении, даже и разглядеть нельзя было хорошенько; другой же угол был уже слишком безобразно тупой. Во всей этой большой комнате почти совсем не было мебели. В углу, направо, находилась кровать; подле нее, ближе к двери, стул. По той же стене, где была кровать, у самых дверей в чужую квартиру, стоял простой тесовый стол, покрытый синенькою скатертью; около стола два плетеных стула. Затем, у противоположной стены, поблизости от острого угла, стоял небольшой, простого дерева комод, как бы затерявшийся в пустоте. Вот все, что было в комнате. Желтоватые, обшмыганные и истасканные обои почернели по всем углам; должно быть, здесь бывало сыро и угарно зимой. Бедность была видимая; даже у кровати не было занавесок.[20]

(It was a big but extremely low-ceilinged room, the only one let by the Kapernaumovs, the locked door to whose apartment was in the wall to the left. Opposite, in the right-hand wall, there was another door, always tightly shut. This led to another, adjoining apartment with a different number. Sonya's room had something barnlike about it; it was of a very irregular rectangular shape, which gave it an ugly appearance. A wall with three windows looking onto the canal cut somehow obliquely across the room, making one corner, formed of a terribly acute angle, run somewhere into the depths where, in the weak light, it could not even be seen very well; the other corner was too grotesquely obtuse. The whole big room had almost no furniture in it. There was a bed in the corner to the right; a chair next to it, nearer the door. Along the same wall as the bed, just by the door to the other apartment, stood a simple wooden table covered with a dark blue cloth and, at the table, two rush-bottom chairs. Then, against the opposite wall, near the acute corner, there was a small chest of drawers, made of plain wood, standing as if lost in the emptiness. That was all there was in the room. The

---

20 Dostoevskii, *Sobranie sochinenii v 15 tomakh*, 5:305.

yellowish, frayed, and shabby wallpaper was blackened in all the corners; it must have been damp and fumy in winter. The poverty was evident; there were not even any curtains over the bed.)[21]

This room shares several attributes with the decaying rooms of Old Grandet: irregularity of spaces, a general sense of gloom and decay, and yellowing wallpaper that is even darker in the corners, indicating the lack of any upkeep. Sonya's drab walls evoke the dark fly spots on the wallpaper of Grandet's main hall, and even her rush-bottom chairs are made of the same material as Madame Grandet and Eugénie's light work chairs. The mysterious door that is always locked leads to the apartment of Svidrigailov, and one is reminded of the always-closed door to the office of Old Grandet where he kept his money and worked alone on his sinister financial deals.

Following Balzac, Dostoevsky repeatedly connects his characters' living quarters to their inner world. Further, as Joel Hunt points out in his article "Color Imagery in Dostoevskij and Balzac," Dostoevsky transforms Balzac's tradition of symbolic descriptions in accordance with his moral, aesthetic, and theological views.[22] Imbued with moral and psychological connotations, the resulting descriptions make the buildings resemble living and feeling creatures. In the description of Rogozhin's house in *The Idiot*, when Prince Myshkin first visits Rogozhin in Saint Petersburg, Dostoevsky even uses Balzac's word *physionomie* talking about Rogozhin's house:

Один дом, вероятно, по своей особенной физиономии, еще издали стал привлекать его внимание, и князь помнил потом, что сказал себе: "Это наверно тот самый дом." С необыкновенным любопытством подходил он проверить свою догадку; он чувствовал, что ему почему-то будет особенно неприятно, если он угадал. Дом этот был большой, мрачный, в три этажа, без всякой архитектуры, цвету грязно-зеленого. Некоторые, очень впрочем немногие дома в этом роде, выстроенные в конце прошлого столетия, уцелели именно в этих улицах Петербурга (в котором всё так скоро меняется) почти без перемены. Строены они прочно, с толстыми стенами и с чрезвычайно редкими окнами; в нижнем этаже окна иногда с решетками. Большею частью внизу меняльная лавка. Скопец, заседающий в лавке, нанимает вверху. И снаружи, и внутри, как-то негостеприимно и сухо, всё как будто скрывается и

21 Dostoevsky, *Crime and Punishment*, 315.
22 Joel Hunt, "Color Imagery in Dostoevskij and Balzac," *Slavic and East European Journal* 10, no. 4 (Winter 1966): 411.

таится, а почему так кажется по одной физиономии дома,—было бы трудно объяснить. Архитектурные сочетания линий имеют, конечно, свою тайну. В этих домах проживают почти исключительно одни торговые. Подойдя к воротам и взглянув на надпись, князь прочел: "Дом потомственного почетного гражданина Рогожина."[23]

(One house, probably because of its odd physiognomy, began to attract his attention while he was still some way off, and the prince remembered later that he said to himself: "This must be the house." With intense curiosity, he went closer to verify his guess; he felt that for some reason he would find it particularly unpleasant if his guess proved to be correct. The house was large, gloomy, three storeys high, without any architectural merit, a dirty green color. Some houses in this genre, though very few in number, built at the end of the last century, have survived in precisely these streets of St. Petersburg [in which everything alters so quickly] nearly unaltered. They are built solidly, with thick walls and exceedingly few windows; on the ground floor the windows sometimes have bars. Usually the ground floor is taken by a moneychanger's shop. The skopets, who sits in the shop, rents the floor above. Both outside and inside the place feels somehow inhospitable and arid, everything appears to be screening and concealing itself, but why it seems this way purely from the house's physiognomy would be hard to explain. Architectural combinations of lines have their secret, of course. These houses are almost exclusively inhabited by tradesfolk. As he approached the gates and glanced at the inscription, the prince read: "The House of Hereditary Distinguished Burgher Rogozhin")[24]

In the description of Rogozhin's house, there are several details echoing the look of the house of Old Grandet. Both houses are described as relics, which somehow have survived into the present. Both share the massive and substantial build and solidity, along with the general impression of gloom and darkness. Both have grills—Grandet's house on the heavy old door and Rogozin's house on the lower windows, evoking associations of prison. The overall impression of ugliness and chaos (*bezobrazie*) that is so central for Dostoevsky's Saint Petersburg spaces is emphasized here. Because of that unpleasant sensation created by the house, Prince Myshkin says to

---

23 Dostoevskii, *Sobranie sochinenii v 12 tomakh*, 6:217.
24 Dostoevsky, *The Idiot*, trans. David McDuff (London: Penguin, 2004), 239.

Rogozhin that he could guess his house even from a hundred paces away. When Rogozhin asks how that is possible, Prince Myshkin answers:

> —Не знаю совсем. Твой дом имеет физиономию всего вашего семейства и всей вашей рогожинской жизни, а спроси, почему я этак заключил,— ничем объяснить не могу. Бред, конечно. Даже боюсь, что это меня так беспокоит. Прежде и не вздумал бы, что ты в таком доме живешь, а как увидал его, так сейчас и подумалось: "да ведь такой точно у него и должен быть дом !"[25]

> (—I really don't know. Your house bears the physiognomy of your whole family and the whole of your Rogozhin way of life, but ask why I came to that conclusion, and I can't explain it. It is a delirium, of course. I am even frightened that it troubles me so much. Before it could have never crossed my mind that you would live in a house like this, but as soon as I caught sight of it, I at once thought: "Why, but that's exactly the sort of house he'd be bound to have!")[26]

Just as in the description of Old Grandet's house, the reader is immediately immersed in an atmosphere of gloom, melancholy, darkness, and emptiness. Moreover, it is significant for Dostoevsky's aesthetics and moral values that the ground floor of Rogozhin's house and the houses of "that kind" are typically occupied by pawnbrokers, who for both, Balzac and Dostoevsky, represent the concentration of evil and misery, and the hidden power of money. This is why Prince Myshkin feels so ill at ease, if he guessed right when wondering whether the house belonged to Rogozhin.

Many biographers[27] point out that in his personal life Balzac appreciated beautiful furnishing and objects, and was an avid collector of antiques. Many novels in *La Comédie humaine* vividly describe the richness and opulence of chic Parisian apartments and houses of the aristocracy of Saint-Germain-des-Prés. In *Eugénie Grandet,* however, there is no description of the Parisian apartment of Charles or of Old Grandet's brother. Rather, Balzac's attention is focused solely on the aging and austere house in Saumur. The hints of the lost luxuries only appear when Charles's luggage

---

25 Dostoevskii, *Sobranie sochinenii v 15 tomakh*, 6:220.
26 Dostoevsky, *The Idiot*, 242.
27 Stefan Zweig, *Balzac*, trans. William Rose, Dorothy Rose, and Richard Friedenthal (New York: Viking, 1946).

is brought in, seen through the eyes of Eugénie, who is fascinated by the brilliant, beautiful objects that she has never seen before.

In Balzac's world, accessories, clothes, and furnishings function as a code that helps to reveal the characters' motives and actions, and this code must be interpreted by the reader. Dostoevsky, by contrast, is always more interested in *bezobrazie* (ugliness)[28] and his attention as a writer is concentrated on depicting ugly and impoverished spaces. These are recreated with painstaking detail, while objects of beauty and luxury are described in much less detail and in very general terms. The concept of *bezobrazie* in Dostoevsky's poetics reflects not only a lack of aesthetic value but also moral critique of an object or a person, connecting it to the Eastern Orthodox symbolism of *obraz*—the image of God. This will be discussed in greater detail later in this chapter.

Faces in Balzac's and Dostoevsky's Texts in the Context of Theory of Physiognomy

Balzac's attention is always focused on crafting detailed and precise portraits of his characters. His creative approach to describing faces, clothes, and the movements of his characters reflects his great interest in Johann Kasper Lavater's (1741–1801) theory of physiognomy,[29] very popular in the nineteenth century among educated European audiences. Lavater's theory of physiognomy, which suggested the correlation of character with facial features and body shape, was very influential in Balzac's Paris, and it was used as the basis of many medical, psychological, and anthropological theories of the day.

Physiognomy as a field of inquiry has a long history, starting with ancient Greek philosophers. Lavater based his theory on a work attributed to Aristotle, *Of the Judgement of Physiognomy*, that first connected certain physical features with moral qualities. Later Giambattista della Porta also wrote about physiognomy in his treatise in Latin *De humana physiognomonia* (1586), accompanying his work with extensive illustrations that highlighted the resemblance of certain facial types to animals. His study of human and animal similitude continued Aristotle's theory, and also

---

28 For more see Robert Louis Jackson, *Dostoevsky's Quest for Form: A Study of His Philosophy of Art* (New Haven, CT: Yale University Press, 1966), 58.

29 Judith Wechsler, *A Human Comedy: Physiognomy and Caricature in 19th-Century Paris* (Chicago: University of Chicago Press, 1982)

caught the attention of Lavater later on. Lavater wrote three volumes of his *Physiognomische Fragmente zur Beförderung der Menschenkenntnis und Menschenliebe* and illustrated it with hundreds of plates of famous historical figures, demonstrating how the shape of the skull or the size of the nose or the chin correlated with certain character traits. Lavater believed that habitual emotions and feelings were manifested over time on a person's face, and this belief led him to state that "Often repeated states of the mind give hability. Habits are derived from propensities and generate passions. . . . The beauty and deformity of the countenance is in just and determinate proportion to the moral beauty and deformity of the man. The morally best, the most beautiful. The morally worst, the most deformed."[30]

Balzac, like many of his contemporaries, was avidly interested in the subject and studied it; he had in his library the annotated French edition, prepared by Moreau de la Sartre, of Lavater's multi-volume treatise *Essai sur la physionomie, destiné à faire connoître l'homme et à le faire aimer*. Moreover, Balzac often mentioned Lavater's ideas in his writing.[31] In his *Physiologie du mariage* Balzac acknowledged that "Physiognomy has created a real science, which has taken its place at last among human knowledge."[32] In *Une Ténébreuse affaire*, he stressed that "the laws of physiognomy are exact, not only as they apply to character, but also as they apply to the destined course in life."[33] Physiognomy of faces of the Parisians, eloquently expressing their vices, thoughts, and desires, is pursued explicitly in the opening of *La Fille aux yeux d'or*.[34] Stefan Zweig in his comparative study *Balzac, Dickens, Dostoevsky: Master Builders of the Spirit* especially noted Balzac's mastery of physiognomic observation, saying that for Balzac

> a face was a stone tablet whereon the life-will had placed its sign manual. And, just as geologists are able to tell the story of a whole epoch by studying the lesson of the rocks and the fossils to be found therein, so, Balzac contended, should an imaginative writer be able by studying faces to decipher the character and the inner possibilities of men.[35]

---

30 Johann Caspar Lavater, *Essays on Physiognomy*, trans. Thomas Holcroft (London and New York: Ward, Lock, 1804), 99.
31 Wechsler, *A Human Comedy*, 25.
32 Ibid., 24.
33 Ibid., 26.
34 Honoré de Balzac, *La Fille aux yeux d'or* (Lausanne: Éditions Rencontre, 1968), 6.
35 Zweig, *Balzac, Dickens, Dostoevsky: Master Builders of the Spirit*, 34.

Later, similar ideas were expressed by the Italian physician, criminologist, and the founder of Italian school of positivist criminology, Cesare Lombroso (1835–1901). Lombroso believed that a person's predisposition to committing a crime could be identified by certain physical atavistic traits manifested in his or her appearance (sloping forehead, asymmetry in the face, long arms, protruding forward jawline, and so forth). According to Lomroso's theory, these features were preserved in certain types of men, establishing the link with primates and encouraging them to behave in similar savage ways. He based his descriptive studies on numerous precise measurements of skulls and size of brains. After his death, his own skull was measured and his head preserved, following his instructions.

Another important contributor to the theory of physiognomy was Franz Joseph Gall (1758–1828). Gall was the pioneer of phrenology or craniology—a related theory that looked for the manifestation of personality traits in the shape of a person's skull, where the cranial bumps located in certain places were indicative of specific personality traits and intellectual abilities. After Gall's lecture tour from 1805 to 1807, phrenology became very popular in Europe, and in 1828, the Phrenological Society of Paris, which included many influential medical school professors among its members, was founded. This society was very active in the period of 1828–1848, just as Balzac was working on his novels.[36] Researchers estimated that Balzac quoted Lavater or Gall more than a hundred times in *La Comédie humaine*.[37]

Lavater's controversial work sparked great interest in physiognomic theory among the novelists of the nineteenth century. Gall's ideas were very influential in Russia, and Dostoevsky was also familiar with his work. According to the memoirs of Dr. Yanovsky,[38] a family physician and close friend of Dostoevsky, Dostoevsky's visits to Yanovsky included study of the illustrations to Gall's famous book *Anatomie et physiologie du système nerveaux* (1819). Analyzing the shape of Dostoevsky's skull according to Gall's system, his doctor compared the shape of his head to Socrates, and

---

36 Jason Y Hall, "Gall's Phrenology: A Romantic Psychology," *Studies in Romanticism* 16, no. 3: *Romanticism and Science* (Summer 1977): 305–317.

37 Christopher Rivers, *Face Value: Physiognomical Thought and the Legible Body in Marivaux, Lavater, Balzac, Gautier, and Zola* (Madison, WI: University of Wisconsin Press, 1994).

38 James L. Rice, *Dostoevsky and the Healing Art: An Essay in Literary and Medical History* (New York: Ardis, 1985), 122.

Dostoevsky was very pleased with that comparison.[39] Dostoevsky also read Carl Gustav Carus (1789–1869) who developed Gall's and Lavater's ideas further in his *Cranioscopie* (1841); and even made plans to translate Carus's *Psyche* (1846) into Russian. In *Psyche*, Carus discusses his concepts of the bodily-psychic connection and the theory of the unconscious. Thus, the ideas of Lavater and Gall were also very much present in Dostoevsky's creative approach as he shaped the portraits of his characters later on.

Following Gall's and Lavater's approach that stressed the connection between appearance and moral character, Balzac focuses on certain facial features of Grandet indicating particular traits of his personality, as he creates the following eloquent portrait in the beginning of *Eugénie Grandet*:

> Au physique, c'était un homme de cinq pieds, trapu, carré, ayant des mollets de douze pouces de circonférence, des rotules noueuses et larges épaules. Son visage était rond, tanné, marqué de petites-vérole. Son menton était droit, ses lèvres, sans sinuosités, et ses dents blanches. Ses yeux avaient l'expression calme et dévoratrice que le vulgaire accorde au basilic. Son front, plein de rides transversales, ne manquait pas de protubérances significatives. Ses cheveux jaunâtres et grisonnants étaient *blanc et or*, disaient quelque jeunes gens qui ne connaissaient pas la gravité d'une plaisanterie faite sur M.Grandet. Son nez, gros par le bout, supportait une loupe venéee que le vulgaire disait, non sans raison, pleine de malice. En somme, sa figure annonçait une finesse dangereuse, une probité sans chaleur, et l'egoisme d'un homme habitué à concentrer ses sentiments dans la jouissance de l'avarice, et sur le seul être qui lui fût réellement de quelque chose, sa fille, Eugénie, sa seule héritière. Attitude, manières, démarche, tout en lui, d'ailleurs, attestait cette croyance en soi que donne l'habitude d'avoir toujours réussi dans ses enterprises. Aussi, quoique de meurs faciles et molles en apparence, M. Grandet avait-il un caractère de bronze.[40]

> (Physically Grandet was five feet in height, thick-set, square, with twelve-inch calves, bony knees, and broad shoulders. His face was round, sunburned, and pitted with smallpox. His chin was straight, his lips thin, and his teeth white. His eyes had the calm, voracious expression that people ascribe to the basilisk. His forehead, crossed by innumerable lines, was not without significant bumps. His yellowish, graying hair was like *silver and gold*, said

---

39 Ibid.
40 Balzac, *Eugénie Grandet*, 42.

some of the young people who did not realize the impropriety of making fun of Monsieur Grandet. His nose, thick at the tip, bore a veined wen, which the common herd said, not without reason, was full of malice. This face revealed a dangerous cunning, a calculated integrity,[41] the egoism of a man accustomed to limit his emotions to the joys of avarice and to the only being who really meant anything to him, his daughter Eugénie, his sole heiress. Attitude, manners, bearing, in short everything about him, demonstrated the complete assurance that comes from unvarying success in all one's undertakings. Thus, though his manners were easy and soft outwardly, Monsieur Grandet's character was that of iron.)[42]

In this portrait several important details are mentioned. First, the color and shape of the eyes are extremely significant in Lavater's theory of physiognomy. Balzac compares the expression of Grandet's eyes to the basilisk's deadly stare, which has the meaningful connotation of hidden danger and death. Merriam-Webster's dictionary gives the following definition: "In Hellenic and Roman legend a basilisk (also called a cockatrice) was a serpent-like creature capable of destroying other creatures by way of its deadly stare."[43] Balzac's use of this image in the novel suggests a mysterious aura of all-powerful evil lurking behind the outwardly calm appearance of Grandet. The comparison of Grandet to a basilisk and later to a serpent and boa constrictor is characteristic of Balzac's portraiture, where animal imagery was always significant.[44] In *Eugénie Grandet*, the old Grandet is compared on several occasions to a tiger and a serpent, who greedily opens his jaws and swallows the gold, and his faithful servant Nanon is repeatedly compared to a loyal dog, emphasizing her absolute loyalty to her master. Old Madame Grandet is called *biche effrayée* (a frightened doe), *un agneau sans tâche* (an innocent lamb), and *la mouette* (a seagull), evoking the attributes of vulnerability associated with these species.

Balzac's use of animalistic metaphors in his novels also continues the earlier work of Charles Le Brun (1616–1690), who, as a portraitist, studied the analogies between human and animal features and developed a theory establishing a correlation between the human face and the

---

41 "Probity" is a closer equivalent here.

42 Balzac, *Père Goriot, and Eugénie Grandet*, 303.

43 "Basilisk," Merriam-Webster, https://www.merriam-webster.com/dictionary/basilisk.

44 Lawrence W. Lynch, "People, Animals, and Transformations in Eugénie Grandet," *The International Fiction Review*, February 9, 2017, https://journals.lib.unb.ca/index.php/IFR/article/view/13620/14703.

animal characterized by a particular quality.[45] In 1671 in Paris, at the Royal Academy of Painting and Sculpture, Le Brun presented a series of lectures illustrated by his drawings that proved the relationship between human and animal physiognomies. Le Brun's physiognomic plates were published as a separate edition in 1806 in Paris and sparked a great interest in the subject.

In Gall's phrenology, humans are studied in the context of natural history and evolution; like Le Brun, Gall makes repeated comparisons between humans and animals. In fact, twenty of his "fundamental powers" representing emotions and intellectual abilities are shared by humans and animals, and only seven are presented as unique to humans, such as the ability to write poetry and appreciate music. In Balzac's fictional world, animal metaphors are used in addition to physiognomy as a tool to provide another layer to a character's portrait. Acknowledging Balzac's great interest in Gall's phrenology and Lavater's theory of physiognomy, Stefan Zweig noted in his study of Balzac: "Every face he saw was for him [Balzac] a charade to be unriddled. He fancied he could discern a likeness to some animal in every one of them; thought he could detect the signs which pointed to an early death; boasted that he could guess the profession of any passer-by through a study of externals of gait and clothing."[46]

Another memorable detail of Old Grandet's portrait is the "significant bumps" on his forehead. This descriptive element is a direct reference to Gall's theory of phrenology. Gall's theory stated that moral and intellectual faculties are innate, not acquired, and that they are visibly manifested in the shape of a person's head. The location of cranial bumps, he argued, was indicative of specific personality traits. In light of Gall's theory, Balzac places certain prominent bumps on Grandet's head to indicate to his readers, also familiar with phrenology, Grandet's main character traits—his strong sense of property, cunning in business, and firmness.

The prominent bumps on Old Grandet's skull indicating his moral qualities did not go unnoticed by the young Dostoevsky, who was also familiar with Gall's and Lavater's works. In his translation, Dostoevsky refers to "remarkable bumps," but he makes several changes in his portrait.

С виду Гранде был футов пяти ростом, плотный и здоровый. Ноги его были двенадцати дюймов в окружности; мускулист и широкоплеч.

---

45 Michel Gareau and Lydia Beauvais, *Charles Le Brun. First Painter to King Louis XIV* (New York: Abrams, 1992).
46 Zweig, *Balzac, Dickens, Dostoevsky: Master Builders of the Spirit*, 36.

Лицо круглое и рябоватое. Подбородок его был прямой, губы тонкие и ровные, зубы белые. Взгляд мягкий, ласковый, жадный, взгляд василиска. Лоб, изрезанный морщинами, с замечательными выпуклостями. Волосы его желтели и седели, все в одно время—*золото и серебро*, по выражению охотников пошутить, вероятно не знавших, что с Гранде не шутят. На толстом носу его висела красная шишка, в которой иные люди склонны были усматривать тайное коварство. Целое выражало тихость сомнительную, холодную честность и эгоизм скупца. Замечали еще в нем одно—привязанность, любовь к своей дочери Евгении, единственной наследнице. Походка, приемы выражали самоуверенность, удачу во всем; и действительно, Гранде, хоть тихий и уклончивый, был твердого, железного характера.[47]

(In appearance Grandet was five feet tall, stocky and healthy. His calves were twelve inches in circumference; he was muscular and broad-shouldered. His face was round and pockmarked. His chin was straight, his lips thin, his teeth were straight and white. His stare was soft, tender, greedy, the stare of a basilisk. His forehead, cut across by wrinkles, had remarkable bulges. His hair turned yellow and white, all at the same time—*gold and silver*, joked some merry-makers who probably did not know that one does not joke with Grandet. On his nose hung a thick red bump in which some people were inclined to see secret cunning. His whole expression conveyed deceptive calm, cold honesty and the selfishness of a miser. People noticed in him one more thing—his attachment, his love for his daughter Eugenia, his sole heiress. His gait, his movements expressed self-confidence, and luck in everything; and indeed, Grandet, though quiet and evasive, possessed a firm, iron character.)[48]

Here Dostoevsky adds some epithets describing Old Grandet, such as inserting "tender" into the row of epithets for his "basilisk stare." In the translation, the stare of Grandet is described as soft, tender, and greedy (*мягкий, ласковый и жадный*), colliding seemingly opposing attributes and highlighting the hidden danger that lurks under Grandet's seemingly soft exterior. Dostoevsky further emphasizes the sternness of Grandet: in addition to saying that Grandet was a man of iron character Dostoevsky adds yet another adjective *твердый*—"firm." In the last sentence, Balzac's

---

47 Dostoevskii, *Evgeniia Grande*, 16.
48 Translation mine.

wordplay contrasting Grandet's outward softness of manners and his iron character is lost in Russian, since in Russian translation the word "soft" (*molle*) is replaced with "quiet" (*тихий*). In Balzac's original, Grandet has the egoism of a man who is used to concentrate his feelings in the joy of avarice—"l'egoisme d'un homme habitué à concentrer ses sentiments dans la jouissance de l'avarice." Dostoevsky shortens this by saying only that Grandet had the selfishness of a miser, which simplifies Balzac's characteristic and eliminates the implied allusion to Grandet's sexual pleasure presumably derived from amassing the gold.

In creating his own characters, Dostoevsky returned many times to the application of physiognomy and phrenology, the use of which he observed in Balzac's text. In *The Idiot*, Prince Myshkin first hears of Nastasya Filippovna's remarkable beauty as he listens to Rogozhin on a train; then sees her photograph shown to him by General Yepanchin and Ganya. The third time, he actually sees her in person and is able to recognize her from her picture. Her appearance in the photograph is described in very general terms:

> На портрете была изображена действительно необыкновенной красоты женщина. Она была сфотографирована в черном шелковом платье, чрезычайно простого и изящного фасона; волосы, по-видимому темно-русые, были убраны просто, по-домашнему; глаза темные, глубокие, лоб задумчивый; выражение лица страстное и как бы высокомерное. Она была несколько худа лицом, может быть, и бледна....[49]

> (The portrait really did depict a woman of unusual beauty. She had been photographed in a black silk dress of exceedingly simple and elegant cut; her hair, apparently dark russet, was done up simply, in domestic fashion; her eyes were dark and deep, her forehead pensive; the expression of her face was passionate and slightly haughty. She was somewhat thin in the face, perhaps, and pale....)[50]

In this portrait no specific features are mentioned, except for general comments about her pale and thin face and dark eyes, as well as her simply cut, elegant black dress that can be viewed as a symbol of mourning. Prince

---

49 Dostoevskii, *Sobranie sochinenii v 15 tomakh*, 6:33.
50 Dostoevsky, *The Idiot*, 36.

Myshkin continues to study the photograph for some time and says, summarizing his observation:

> Удивительное лицо!—ответил князь,—и я уверен, что судьба ее не из обыкновенных. Лицо веселое, а она ведь ужасно страдала, а? Об этом глаза говорят, вот эти две косточки, две точки под глазами в начале щек. Это гордое лицо, ужасно гордое, и вот не знаю, добра ли она? Ах, кабы добра! Все было бы спасено![51]

> ("An astonishing face!" the prince replied. "And I am certain that her fate is not of an ordinary kind. Her face is cheerful, but she has suffered dreadfully, don't you think? Her eyes betray it, those two little bones here, two points under her eyes where her cheeks begin. It's a proud face, a dreadfully proud one, and I simply can't tell if she is good or not. If only she was good! Everything would be saved.)[52]

Interestingly, Prince Myshkin's description of Nastasya Filippovna is more specific than her previous portrait given by the narrator, and Myshkin even mentions "two little bones" on her face that indicate that she has suffered a lot. In fact, Prince Myshkin's uncanny ability to read faces is mentioned explicitly several times in the novel. For example, when he first visits the Yepanchins, the mother talks to him about her daughters, saying that their teasing is not malicious and that she knows their faces.

> Они, верно, что-нибудь затеяли, но они уже вас любят. Я их лица знаю.
> —И я их лица знаю,—сказал князь, особенно ударяя на свои слова.
> —Это как?—спросила Аделаида с любопытством.
> —Что вы знаете про наши лица?—залюбопытствовали и две другие.
> Но князь молчал и был серьезен; все ждали его ответа.
> —Я вам после скажу,—сказал он тихо и серьезно.[53]

("They've probably got something up their sleeve, but they already like you. I know by their faces."

"I know by their faces, too," said the prince, giving his words particular emphasis.

"How can that be?" Aglaya asked with curiosity.

---

51 Dostoevskii, *Sobranie sochinenii v 15 tomakh*, 6:39.
52 Dostoevsky, *The Idiot*, 43.
53 Dostoevskii, *Sobranie sochinenii v 15 tomakh*, 6:72.

"What do you know about our faces?" the two others also asked
curiously.

But the prince said nothing, and looked earnest; they all awaited his
reply.

"I'll tell you later," he said quietly and earnestly.)[54]

In this short exchange, Prince Myshkin demonstrates his distinctive sensitivity, his delicacy of feeling, and perspicacity that allows him to make
profound and accurate observations on people that he meets, despite his
aura of child-like innocence and naiveté. Dostoevsky makes his protagonist a skilled reader of physiognomy, even though his interlocutor Madame
Yepanchin jokes about her own ability to read her daughters' faces.

Dostoevsky and the Poetics of Ugliness

Dostoevsky shares Balzac's interest in the physical settings of his novels.
Yet, he differs from Balzac in that he never provides a detailed description of beautiful interiors or of the latest fashions and styles. He chooses
instead to concentrate his attention on the description of the most poor
and squalid features of the interiors, clothes, and faces and paints striking
images of *bezobrazie* (ugliness). *Bezobrazie* in Russian morphologically literally means the state of being "without an image." Significantly, the word
for an icon in Russian is *obraz*, so being "without an image" also means
being "without God." Lack of moral goodness and physical manifestations
of ugliness are strongly linked in Dostoevsky's world. Robert Jackson in
his analyses of beauty in Dostoevsky's aesthetics points out that "the mor-
al-aesthetic spectrum of Dostoevsky begins with *obraz*—image, form and
embodiment of beauty—and ends with *bezobrazie*—literally that which is
'without image,' shapeless, disfigured, ugly. . . . Aesthetically, *bezobrazie* is
the deformation of ideal form (*obraz*)."[55]

Fyodor Karamazov embodies in his character all aspects of *bezobrazie*—from physical ugliness to debauchery and violence. In *Brothers
Karamazov*, Dostoevsky creates a very long and specific description of
Fyodor Karamazov, his bushy eyebrows, his nose, repeatedly emphasizing
the ugliness of his appearance:

---

54 Dostoevsky, *The Idiot*, 78.
55 Jackson, *Dostoevsky's Quest for Form*, 58.

Я уже говорил, что он очень обрюзг. Физиономия его представляла к тому времени что-то резко свидетельствующее о характеристике и сущности всей прожитой им жизни. Кроме длинных и мясистых мешочков под маленькими его глазами, вечно наглыми, подозрительными и насмешливыми, кроме множества глубоких морщинок на его маленьком, на жирненьком личике, к острому его подбородку подвешивался еще большой кадык, мясистый и продолговатый, как кошелек, что придавало ему какой-то отвратительно сладострастный вид. Прибавьте к этому плотоядный, длинный рот, с пухлыми губами, из-под которых виднелись маленькие обломки черных, почти истлевших зубов. Он брызгался слюной каждый раз, когда начинал говорить.[56]

(I have already mentioned that he had grown very bloated. His physiognomy by that time presented something that testified acutely to the characteristics and essence of his whole life. Besides the long, fleshy bags under his eternally insolent, suspicious, and leering little eyes, besides the multitude of deep wrinkles on his fat little face, a big Adam's apple, fleshy and oblong like a purse, hung below his sharp chin, giving him a sort of repulsively sensual appearance. Add to that long, carnivorous mouth with plump lips, behind which could be seen the little stumps of black, almost decayed teeth. He sprayed saliva whenever he spoke.)[57]

Fyodor Karamazov's physical portrait is the most complete and defined one in *The Brothers Karamazov*. It is full of significant details: the narrator states explicitly that Fyodor Karamazov's face bears a testimony of sorts to the type of life that he led, indirectly evoking the principles of Lavater's theory of physiognomy, which were discussed earlier in this chapter in connection with Balzac's works. Similarly, Smerdyakov, Fyodor's illegitimate son, who is also morally corrupt and is responsible for his father's murder, is portrayed in great detail, focusing on the elements of *bezobrazie* manifested in his appearance. The reader is given a physical description of Smerdyakov when he becomes a young man, after first reading about his predilection to violent games as a child and his fits of epilepsy:

---

56 Dostoevskii, *Sobranie sochinenii v 15 tomakh*, 6: 28.

57 Fyodor Dostoyevsky, *The Brothers Karamazov: A Novel in Four Parts with Epilogue*, trans. Richard Pevear and Larissa Volokhonsky (New York: Random House, 1991), 23.

В ученье он пробыл несколько лет и воротился, сильно переменившись лицом. Он вдруг как-то необычайно постарел, совсем даже несоразмерно с возрастом сморщился, пожелтел, стал походить на скопца. Нравственно же воротился почти тем же самым, как и до отъезда в Москву: все так же был нелюдим и ни в чьем обществе не ощущал ни малейшей надобности. [58]

(He spent a few years in training, and came back much changed in appearance. He suddenly became somehow remarkably old, with wrinkles even quite disproportionate to his age, turned sallow, and began to look like a eunuch. But morally he was almost the same when he returned as he had been before his departure for Moscow, was still just as unsociable, and felt not the slightest need for anyone's company).[59]

In keeping with the theory of physiognomy, Dostoevsky makes his morally repulsive character also very unattractive in appearance by drawing the readers' attention to Smerdyakov's unusually old and sallow face, wrinkled beyond his years, and his overall look resembling a eunuch. That comparison implies not only the absence of vitality and vigor, but also connotes sickness and disrepute from violating life's essential laws.

The good-looking characters in *The Brothers Karamazov* are described in a much more general manner. For example, regarding Alyosha's appearance, readers only know that he was handsome and resembled his mother who is described vaguely as having "remarkable beauty" and "innocent looks." Dostoevsky's exceptional attention to the portraits of Fyodor Karamazov and Smerdyakov indicate that he had a great interest in the physical embodiment of *bezobrazie* and, like Balzac, insisted on a correlation of physical appearance and morality. For Dostoevsky, who was focused mostly on the inner workings of the dark sides of human nature, beautiful faces presented considerably less interest, and he chose to focus his attention instead on the physical and moral ugliness instead.

In *The Idiot*, Nastasya Filippovna's appearance is presented only in general terms as "extremely beautiful." Similarly, the three Yepanchin sisters are portrayed in rather vague manner as "healthy, blossoming, tall, with striking shoulders, powerful bosoms, strong arms."[60] Aglaya, the youngest of the sisters, who falls in love with Prince Myshkin, is only described as "the

---

58 Dostoevskii, *Sobranie sochinenii v 15 tomakh*, 11:148.
59 Dostoevsky, *The Brothers Karamazov*, 125.
60 Dostoevsky, *The Idiot*, 43.

most beautiful of the three." Rogozhin's face, on the other hand, is depicted in great detail:

> Один из них был небольшого роста, лет двадцати семи, курчавый и почти черноволосый, с серыми маленькими, но огненными глазами. Нос его был широк и сплюснут, лицо скуластое, тонкие губы беспрерывно складывались в какую-то наглую, насмешливую и даже злую улыбку; но лоб его был высок и хорошо сформирован и скрашивал неблагородно развитую нижнюю челюсть лица. Особенно приметна была в этом лице его мертвая бледность, придававшая всей физиономии молодого человека изможденный вид, несмотря на довольно крепкое сложение, и вместе с тем что-то страстное, до страдания, не гармонировавшее с нахальною и грубою улыбкой и с резким, самодовольным его взглядом.[61]

> One of them was rather short, about twenty-seven, with almost black curly hair, and small, gray, but fiery eyes. His nose was broad and flat, and he had high cheekbones, his thin lips were constantly creased in a kind of brazen, mocking and even cruel smile; but his brow was high and well-formed and did much to compensate for the ignobly developed lower part of his face. Especially striking in that face was its deathly pallor, which gave the whole of the young man's physiognomy an emaciated look, in spite of his rather sturdy build, at the same time imparting to it something passionate, to the point of suffering, that was out of harmony with his coarse and insolent smile and his harsh, self-satisfying gaze.)[62]

The reader is given many specific details about Rogozhin's appearance: the shape and color of Rogozhin's eyes; his short and flat nose, which in physiognomy signals a quick temper; and high forehead, indicating intelligence, to "compensate for the ignobly developed lower part of his face." To describe the face as "ignoble" is to reference directly Lavater's system of face classification. Moreover, in Lavater's theory of physiognomy dark curly hair points to passion, as do small fiery eyes.

For Lavater, the characteristics of the eyes—their color, size, and shape—were one of the most important indicators in interpreting a person's character: "The finest eyes are those which we imagine to be black or blue. Vivacity and fire, which are the principle characteristics of the eyes,

---

61 Dostoevskii, *Sobranie sochinenii v 15 tomakh*, 6: 6.

62 Dostoevsky, *The Idiot*, 6.

are the more emitted when the colors are deep and contrasted, rather than slightly shaded. Black eyes have most strength of expression, and most vivacity; but the blue have most mildness, and, perhaps, are more arch."[63] Significantly, Prince Myshkin's eyes are clear blue suggesting "a great capacity and extreme sensibility and curious inquiry."[64] Lavater also states that "blue eyes are, generally, more significant of weakness, effeminacy, and yielding than brown or black."[65]

In contrast with the very detailed description of Rogozhin's face, considerably less detail is provided about Prince Myshkin's appearance:

> Обладатель плаща с капюшоном был молодой человек, тоже лет двадцати шести или двадцати семи, роста немного повыше среднего, очень белокур, густоволос, со впалыми щеками и с легонькою, востренькою, почти совершенно белою бородкой. Глаза его были большие, голубые и пристальные; во взгляде их было что-то тихое, но тяжелое, что-то полное того странного выражения, по которому некоторые угадывают с первого взгляда в субъекте падучую болезнь. Лицо молодого человека было, впрочем, приятное, тонкое и сухое, но бесцветное, а теперь даже досиня иззябшее.[66]

> (The wearer of the cloak with the hood was a young man, also about twenty-six or twenty-seven, of slightly above average height, with very thick, fair hair, sunken cheeks and a light, pointed, almost completely white little beard. His eyes were large, blue and fixed; in their gaze there was something quiet but heavy and they were filled with that strange expression by which some can detect epilepsy on first glance at a person. The young man's face was, however, pleasant, delicate and lean, though colorless, and now so cold that it was positively blue.)[67]

In complete illustration of Lavater's theory, the epilepsy is manifested in Prince Myshkin's eyes, just as his physical frailty and moral goodness. Myshkin's fine features and paleness coupled with his light blue eyes suggest a general delicacy of feeling and susceptibility. In accordance with Lavater's

---

63 Lavater, *Essays on Physiognomy*, 467.
64 Ibid.
65 Ibid., 383.
66 Dostoevskii, *Sobranie sochinenii v 15 tomakh*, 6:6.
67 Dostoevsky, *The Idiot*, 6.

views, Dostoevsky here focuses specifically on the expression of the eyes. As Lavater wrote,

> The eye appertains more to the soul than any other organ; seems affected by, and participates in all its emotions; expresses sensation the most lively, passion the most tumultuous, feelings the most delightful, and sentiments the most delicate. . . . The eye at once receives and reflects the intelligence of thought, and the warmth of sensibility; it is the sense of the mind, the tongue of the understanding. [68]

Dostoevsky's particular attention to the expression of Myshkin's eyes is evocative of Balzac's technique of portraiture in *Eugénie Grandet* where he also put a particular emphasis on the characters' eye expression. Old Grandet's eyes are famously compared to a basilisk stare, signalling hidden danger. Eugénie's eye expression is compared to that of Raphael's Madonna[69] as a reflection of her inner serenity, capacity for love, and spirituality.

Clothes as Semiotic Signs

In his novels, Balzac always centers his attention on his characters' physical appearance, their clothes, accessories, and small personal items. Expanding Lavater's theory of physical appearance reflecting spiritual qualities of a person, Balzac views clothes as a signifier of the person's inner world. In his "Traité de la vie elégante" he writes, "Pourquoi la toilette serait-elle donc toujours le plus éloquent de style, si elle n'était pas réellement tout l'homme, l'homme avec le texte de son existence, l'homme hiéroglyphié? Aujourd'hui même encore, la vestiognomie est devenue presque une branche de l'art créé par Gall et Lavater"[70] (Why then would the toilet be the most eloquent of style, if it was not really the whole man, the man with the text of his existence, the hieroglyphic man? Even today, vestiognomy has become almost the whole branch of art created by Gall and Lavater).[71] This passage refers to clothes as "eloquent" because in Balzac's view they not only communicate the person's social status but also his or her taste, education, background,

---

68 Lavater, *Essays on Physiognomy*, 386.
69 Dostoevskii, *Evgeniia Grande*, 68.
70 Honoré de Balzac, "Traité de la vie élégante. Physiologie du rentier de Paris," in Honoré de Balzac, Louis Lumet, Honoré Daumier, and Paul Gavarni, *Curiosités Littéraires et Pages Inconnues* (Paris, France: Bibliopolis, 1911).
71 Translation mine.

and many other nuanced personality traits. He even introduces the new term for the study of clothes, *vestiognomie*. Naturally, and in the world of *La Comédie humaine* much can be inferred about the characters and their actions from their clothing choices.

In *Engénie Grandet*, Balzac describes in great detail numerous elegant and fashionable clothes and accessories that young Charles brought from Paris. Among his clothes, there are two coats by Staub, one of the most famous and expensive tailors of Paris of that period, whose services Balzac himself used. To be dressed by Staub was at the time a sure sign of high status. Fine clothes by Staub are mentioned by Stendhal in *Le Rouge et le noire* and by Victor Hugo in *Les Miserables*. The names of Staub and another well-known Parisian tailor, Buisson, appear repeatedly in *La Comédie humaine* as markers of refinement, elegance, and luxury, often attained at great expense and frequently accompanied by going into considerable debt.

The importance of a good tailor cannot be overestimated for success in Paris in the world of *La Comédie humaine*. For example, in *Illusions perdues*, when Lucien arrives in Paris from Angoulême, he first orders his clothes at Buisson's shop and is dismayed when he receives the bill. The tailor reassures him by saying that his trousers made two brilliant marriages, so the expenses incurred at a good tailor should be viewed as an investment in one's brilliant future. Similarly, when Madame de Bargeton arrives in Paris, her savvy friend du Châtelet gives her advice urging her to redo her provincial wardrobe *pour se desangoulêmer* (to lose her "Angouleme" look). Significantly, when Lucien first sees Madame de Bargeton in Paris at the opera box in her provincial evening dress from Angoulême next to her fashionable Parisian relative, he finds her old and ridiculous, while in Angoulême his perception of her and her clothes was very different; he found her very attractive.

In Balzac's novelistic world, clothes serve as a social marker, something that immediately separates the savvy and refined world of Parisian aristocracy from everyone else. He even creates a new verb *se desangoulêmer* to stress the importance of changing one's old provincial habits and views along with one's old outmoded wardrobe. In *Illusions perdues*, this is what follows for Lucien and for Madame de Bargeton: after they have gotten rid of their provincial wardrobes, they both realize that in the new environment each of them no longer finds the other attractive. The change of clothes is the main driving power that facilitates this profound shift in their outlook.

In *Eugénie Grandet,* Balzac creates a stark contrast between the latest Parisian fashion look sported by Charles and the shabby, drab, and worn looks of the residents of Saumur. When Charles first enters the great hall of his uncle, he is struck not only by the old, decaying furnishings and worn upholstery, but also by the slovenly appearance of Grandet's guests. He quickly realizes that his notions of a splendid holiday in the country château of his uncle were utterly unfounded, and he feels completely out of place in his fancy clothes.

> Maintenent, si vous voulez bien comprendre la surprise respective des Saumurois et du jeun Parisien, voir parfaitment la vive lumière que l'élégance du voyageur jetait au milieu des ombres grises de la sale, et des figures qui composaient le tableau de famille, essayez de vous représenter les Cruchots. Touts les trois prenaient du tabac, et ne songaient plus depuis long-temps à éviter ni les roupies, ni pes petites galettes noires don't ils parsemaient le jabot de leurs chemises rousses, à cols recroquevillés et a plis jaunâtre. Leurs cravattes molles se roulaient en corde aussitôt qu'ils se les étaient attachées au cou. L'énorme quantité de linge qui leur permettait de ne faire la lessive que tous les six mois, et de le garder au fond de leurs armoires, permettaient au temps d'y imprimer ses teints grises et vieilles. Il y avait en eux une parfaite entente de mauvaise grâce et de sénilité: leur figures, aussi flêtries que l'étaient leurs habits rapés, aussi plissées que leurs pantalons, semblaient usées, racornies, et grimaçaient.[72]

> (Now if you would understand the mutual surprise of the Saumurois and the young Parisian, and visualize perfectly the radiant gleam cast by the traveler's elegance into the midst of the gray shadows of the hall and of the figures composing this family picture, try and imagine what the Cruchots looked like. All three took snuff, and had long ago ceased to care about the drip from their noses or the little black specks sprinkled over the frills of their dingy shirts with their crumpled collars and yellowing pleats. Their limp cravats twisted into ropes as soon as they tied them round their necks. They had such enormous quantities of linen that they had to have it washed only twice a year; they stored it at the bottom of their cupboards, where time was able to communicate to it its gray and aging hues. These people combined to perfection inelegance and senility. Their faces, as faded as their

---

72 Balzac, *Eugénie Grandet,* 92.

shabby clothes, as wrinkled as their trousers, seemed worn, shriveled and contorted.)[73]

In this description, Balzac ironically mentions the grayish hues of originally white undergarments; shirts, yellowing from time and twice-a-year laundering, covered with black tobacco specks and nose drips; and wrinkled cravats and trousers, which mimic the wrinkled faces. Balzac also uses a sarcastic metaphor saying that in the appearance of the Cruchots one sees *une parfaite entente de mauvaise grâce et de sénilité*—a perfect unity of inelegance and senility. One of his signature conjunctions *aussi . . . que* makes an ironic equation between the worn clothes and the worn faces.

In his translation, Dostoevsky shortens the description, omitting some of the sentences completely and changing others, and loses the mocking intonation of Balzac:

> Теперь, ежели хотите понять почтительное удивление сомюрцев и осветить воображением контраст блистательного денди с сухими, вялыми фигурами гостей в темной, скучной зале Гранде, то взгляните на семейство Крюшо. Все трое нюхали табак, и незаметно привыкли к вечному табачному сору на мелких складках своих пожелтевших манишек. Их галстуки мялись и веревкой обвивались вокруг шеи. Огромный запас белья позволял им, ради хозяйственного расчета, мыть его только два раза в год, отчего белье желтело без употребления в ящиках. Все в них было неловко, некстати, бесцветно; их лица были вялы, сухи и изношены так же, как и их фраки, на которых было столько же складок, как и на панталонах.[74]

(Now, if you want to understand the reverent surprise of the inhabitants of Saumur and allow your imagination to highlight the contrast of the brilliant dandy with the dry, withered figures of the guests in the dark, dull great hall of Grandet, look at the Cruchot family. All three took snuff, and over time got imperceptibly used to the constant tobacco specks on small folds of their yellowed shirt-fronts. Their ties were wrinkled and wrapped in a rope around their neck. Huge stocks of linens allowed them, for the sake of economic calculation, to wash it only twice a year, causing the shirts to yellow in the drawers without use. All of them were awkward, out of place,

---

73 Idem, *Père Goriot, and Eugénie Grandet*, 329.
74 Dostoevskii, *Evgeniia Grande*, 45.

colorless; their faces were as withered, dry and worn out as their coats, which
had as many folds as their trousers.)

In this passage Dostoevsky makes several departures from the French original. He changes "the mutual surprise" of both parties to "reverent surprise
of the residents of Saumur" as they see Charles (*почтительное удивление
сомюрцев*),[75] replaces the "radiant gleam cast by the traveler's elegance into
the midst of the gray shadows of the hall" with "a contrast of brilliant dandy
with dry, lifeless figures of the guests in the dark, boring hall of Grandet"
(*контраст блистательного денди с сухими, вялыми фигурами гостей
в темной, скучной зале Гранде*),[76] and leaves out completely the most
ironic assessment of Balzac: "these people combined to perfection inelegance and senility." These omissions change the ironic caustic tone of Balzac
in describing these two opposite worlds to a serious mood highlighting the
stark opposition of luxurious and young vis-à-vis decaying and old. Not
surprisingly, the Saumur residents feel "respectful surprise" seeing Charles
since he embodies youthful energy and wealth.

The notion of refined elegance is extremely important to Balzac as a
writer and a person. Always interested in fashion, luxury, and beautiful
objects, he fills the fictional world of *La Comédie humaine* with sumptu-
ous, elegant interiors of Parisian boudoirs where young, beautiful women
have clandestine *rendezvous* with their lovers. Balzac's attention is equally
engaged with opulent and with modest interiors, and there is frequently
a contrast between a luxurious and a poor setting in the same novel (*Le
Père Goriot, Gobseck, Splendeurs et misères des courtesans*, and others). For
Balzac, the notion of elegance carries a value judgment, and people lack-
ing elegance also lack taste and general refinement in their sentiments and
mental abilities.

Dostoevsky's focus as a writer is not on elegance *per se* but on a more
abstract, lofty concept of beauty that he links to morality, God, and religious
faith. The word "elegance" is not even mentioned in his writings. However,
the word for luxury—*роскошь*—is used forty-one times.[77] The theme of luxury, its ties to sensual pleasures, and its corrupting effect on morality plays
an important role in Dostoevsky's creation of his *femmes fatales*—Nastasya
Filippovna in *The Idiot* and Grushenka in *The Brothers Karamazov*. In *The*

---

75 Ibid.
76 Ibid.
77 See Iurii Karaulov, ed., *Slovar' iazyka Dostoevskogo* (Moscow, Russia: Azbuka, 2008).

Idiot, when Prince Myshkin first visits Nastasya Filippovna, he is struck by the opulence of her apartment:

Настасья Филипповна занимала не очень большую, но действительно великолепно отделанную квартиру. В эти пять лет ее петербургской жизни было одно время, в начале, когда Афанасий Иванович особенно не жалел для нее денег; он еще рассчитывал тогда на ее любовь и думал соблазнить ее, главное, комфортом и роскошью, зная, как легко прививаются привычки роскоши и как трудно потом отставать от них, когда роскошь мало-помалу обращается в необходимость. В этом случае Тоцкий пребывал верен старым добрым преданиям, не изменяя в них ничего, безгранично уважая всю непобедимую силу чувственных влияний. Настасья Филипповна от роскоши не отказывалась, даже любила ее, но—и это казалось чрезвычайно странным—никак не поддавалась ей, точно всегда могла и без нее обойтись; даже старалась несколько раз заявить о том, что неприятно поражало Тоцкого. Впрочем, многое было в Настасье Филипповне, что неприятно (а впоследствии даже до презрения) поражало Афанасия Ивановича. Не говоря уже о неизящности того сорта людей, которых она иногда приближала к себе, а стало быть, и наклонна была приближать, проглядывали в ней и еще некоторые совершенно странные наклонности: заявлялась какая-то варварская смесь двух вкусов, способность обходиться и удовлетворяться такими вещами и средствами, которых и существование нельзя бы, кажется, было допустить человеку порядочному и тонко развитому.[78]

(Nastasya Filippovna occupied an apartment that was not very large, but magnificently appointed. In these past five years of her life in St. Petersburg there had been a time, at the beginning, when Afanasy Ivanovich was particularly lavish with the money he spent on her; at that time he still had hopes of winning her love, and thought he could seduce her mainly by comfort and luxury, knowing how easily the habits of luxury are acquired and how difficult it is later to give them up, when luxury gradually turns into necessity. From this point of view, Totsky remained faithful to the good old traditions, not changing them in any way, and with a boundless respect for all the invincible power of sensual influences. Nastasya Filipovna did not turn her nose up at luxury, was even fond of it, but—and this seemed exceedingly

---

78 Dostoevskii, *Sobranie sochinenii v 15 tomakh*, 6:146.

strange—in no way surrendered to it, as though she could always manage without it; she even tried to put this into words on this occasion, something that struck Totsky unpleasantly. There were, however, many things about Nastasya Filippovna that struck Afanasy Ivanovich unpleasantly [and subsequently even to the point of the contempt]. Not to speak of the lack of refinement of the class of people she sometimes brought close to herself, and must therefore have been inclined to bring close, there were signs in her of other, quite strange hallucinations: there asserted itself a kind of barbarous mixture of two tastes, a capacity for making do and being content with such things and resources the very existence of which one might have thought no decent and educated person could allow.)[79]

The biography of Nastasya Filippovna has some parallels with Esther from Balzac's *Splendeurs et misères des courtesans*. Like Esther, Nastasia Filippovna is a kept woman who falls in love with someone else, and in the end her love ultimately brings her to her death, though Nastasya Filippovna is murdered by Rogozhin and Esther commits suicide. Nastasya Filippovna's benefactor Tostky tries to make her accustomed to luxury and comforts, to turn it into a habit and necessity of daily living, so that she will not be able to do without luxury and eventually leave him. In this passage, Dostoevsky also mentions the "invincible power of sensual influences," establishing a direct connection between the sensuality connected to the ability to enjoy luxury and comforts and the sensuality and sexuality of human nature, and alluding to the corrupting influence of luxury on morality.

In the case of Nastasya Filippovna, Totsky's expectations of seducing her with luxury were wrong; Totsky says that in Nastasya Filippovna there was "a barbaric mix of two tastes, the ability to exist and be satisfied by such things even existence of which could not be admitted by a decent and refined person." This is a radical departure from Balzac's interpretation of luxury. In Balzac's fictional world, luxury is a great motivator for action, which fuels the ambition of his main characters, such as Eugène de Rastignac and Lucien du Rubempré. Dostoevsky, on the contrary, views luxury as a temptation appealing to one's sensual side, leading people astray and making them forget their principles and duties. For that reason, the notion of luxury ought to be resisted by a person with firm morality and religious faith. Thus, unlike the characters of Balzac, Dostoevsky's Nastasya Filippovna remains immune to the seductive charms of luxury, which

---

79 Dostoyevsky, *The Idiot*, 158.

Totsky counts on to keep her by his side. Her unexpected resistance makes him call her "odd" or "strange" (*странная*).

Like Balzac, Dostoevsky also pays a lot of attention to fashion and clothes, which indicate his characters' social standing. Rather than giving a full-fledged detailed description, as Balzac does, Dostoevsky instead chooses to focus on one or two salient details in the character's clothing or haircut that then become that character's signature elements, such as Sonya's *drap-de-dames* shawl or Luzhin's sideburns or Katerina Ivanovna dreaming of new white embroidered cuffs and collar.

In *Crime and Punishment* the ups and downs in Marmeladov's fate are mirrored in his costume. When after a long period of unemployment he finally gets his job back, his wife Katerina Ivanovna and daughter Sonya are miraculously able to procure a new uniform for him. Marmeladov acknowledges the significance of this action to Raskolnikov when he tells him his story: "How they managed to knock together eleven rubles and fifty kopecks to have me decently outfitted, I don't understand. Boots, cotton shirt fronts—most magnificent, a uniform, they cooked it all up for eleven fifty, in the most excellent aspect, sir."[80] He also notes a great change in Katerina Ivanovna's appearance when he returns from the office for the first time. Her overall look has changed, and she looks younger and prettier: "She does not have any dresses . . . I mean, not any, sir, and there it was as if she were going to a party, all dressed up, and not just in anything, no, she knows how to do it all out of nothing; she fixed her hair, put on some clean collar, some cuffs, and—quite a different person emerged, younger and prettier."[81] As in Balzac's world, a change of wardrobe signifies a change in the character's position in society and indicates new possibilities for a better future. In the story of Marmeladov, these hopes are very short-lived, since he ends up taking his new uniform to the tavern owner in exchange for drinks and dies right afterwards, after being run over by a horse.

Marmeladov's wife, the consumptive and destitute Katerina Ivanovna, reminisces about her happy past life as she tries on the new pretty white collars and cuffs that Lizaveta brought to Sonya. The white cuffs let Katerina Ivanovna forget her tragic circumstances and the squalor of her surroundings for a moment as she looks at them and admires their prettiness and

---

80 Dostoevsky, *Crime and Punishment*, 20.
81 Ibid.

freshness. Sonya remembers this scene after the death of Marmeladov as she talks about Katerina Ivanovna's character to Raskolnikov in her room.

> А Катерине Ивановне очень понравились, она надела и в зеркало посмотрела на себя, и очень, очень ей понравились: "подари мне, говорит, их, Соня, пожалуйста." Пожалуйста попросила, и уж так ей хотелось. А куда ей надевать? Так: прежнее, счастливое время только вспомнилось! Смотрится на себя в зеркало, любуется, и никаких-то, никаких-то у ней платьев нст, никаких-то вещей, вот уж сколько лет! И ничего-то она никогда ни у кого не попросит; гордая, сама скорей отдаст последнее, а вот тут попросила,—так уж ей понравилось![82]

> (And Katerina Ivanovna liked them very much, she put them on and she liked them very, very much. "Sonya, please," she said, "give them to me." She said please, and she wanted them so much. But where would she go in them? She was just remembering her former happy days! She looked in the mirror, admired herself, and she's had no dresses, no dresses at all, no things, for so many years now! And she never asks anything from anybody; she is proud, she'd sooner give away all she has, but this time she asked—she liked them so much!)[83]

Just like Balzac's characters see themselves in a completely different light after they have acquired Parisian clothes, Katerina Ivanovna's whole idealized world of a past life in her parents' house with balls, dresses, and dances suddenly reemerges as she is looking at the new pretty embroidered white cuffs. For Katerina Ivanovna, the cuffs become a symbolic embodiment of her lost world and all the dashed hopes of her youth. The image of white clean linens and undergarments is something that is affixed to Katerina Ivanovna who does laundry every night, almost ritualistically insisting on maintaining that one habit of her comfortable past, where undergarments were spotless and fresh every day. The white cuffs and collar take on a symbolic role representing better things in life and new beginnings. Hence the expression of Katerina's face changes when Sonya reminds her that in her current situation she has no use for them: "А я и отдать пожалела, 'на что вам, говорю, Катерина Ивановна?' Так и сказала, 'на что.' Уж этого-то не надо было ей говорить! Она так на меня посмотрела, и так ей тяжело-тяжело стало, что я отказала, и так это было жалко

---

82 Dostoevskii, *Sobranie sochinenii v 15 tomakh*, 5:309.

83 Dostoevsky, *Crime and Punishment*, 319.

смотреть . . ."[84] (And I grudged giving them to her and said to her: "What do you need them for, Katerina Ivanovna?" That's exactly what I said "what for?" That 'what for?' I should never have said it to her. She just looked at me, and she took it so hard, so hard that I refused, and it was such a pity to see . . .).[85] Reminding Katerina Ivanovna that she has no place to wear the pretty cuffs, Sonya harshly returns Katerina Ivanovna to her present situation, where there is no room for embellishments or dreams, and only physical survival needs are to be struggled with every day.

Clothes as semiotic signs play a similar function in *The Idiot*. In the opening paragraphs of the novel, before Prince Myshkin is introduced, the readers are first told about his enormous European cloak, completely out of place in the carriage and inappropriate for harsh Russian winters. The description of the strange cloak appears even before its wearer is portrayed:

> На нем был довольно широкий и толстый плащ без рукавов и с огромным капюшоном, точь-в-точь как употребляют часто дорожные, по зимам, где-нибудь далеко за границей, в Швейцарии, или например, в Северной Италии, не рассчитывая при этом и на такие концы по дорогое, как от Эйдткунена до Петербурга. Но что годилось и вполне удовлетворяло в Италии, оказалось не совсем пригодным для России.[86]

> (He wore a rather capacious, thick sleeveless cloak with an enormous hood, of the kind often used in winter, in far-off places such as Switzerland or northern Italy, by travellers who do not, of course, have to reckon with the distance between points so far removed as Eidkuhnen and St. Petersburg. But what has been suitable and thoroughly satisfactory in Italy turned out to be not wholly so in Russia).[87]

This conspicuous and extravagant big sleeveless cloak with enormous hood, which looks very exotic in Russia, functions as a prophetic metaphor of sorts for Prince Myshkin's fate in his native land when he returns after a prolonged absence. Prince Myshkin is a European-educated, sensitive idealist who spent many years in Switzerland undergoing treatment for epilepsy. Upon his return to Russia, he finds himself surrounded by foreign and unfamiliar things on many levels, from language and manners to

---

84 Dostoevskii, *Sobranie sochinenii v 15 tomakh*, 5:309.
85 Dostoevsky, *Crime and Punishment*, 320.
86 Dostoevskii, *Sobranie sochinenii v 15 tomakh*, 6:6.
87 Dostoevsky, *The Idiot*, 6.

people's morals and values. Just as his impractical cloak is completely out of place in a frigid car on a Saint Petersburg train, the prince does not fit his social circle in Petersburg. His candor and generosity are perceived as very odd and eccentric by most people. Through this singular detail, Dostoevsky emblematically conveys to the readers the incongruity of his main character. The odd cloak functions as a sign for the events that unfold later in the novel.

This chapter has analyzed several discrepancies that exist between the French original and Dostoevsky's translation of *Eugénie Grandet* focusing specifically on the physical spaces and portrayals of the main characters, and investigated how these changes may be connected to Dostoevsky's own literary style and poetics later on. It demonstrated that Dostoevsky appropriated many creative elements of Balzac's technique that he saw in *Eugénie Grandet*, and incorporated it into his own technique as a writer. Balzac's profound belief in *théorie du milieu* and his life-long interest in Lavater and Gall's theory of physiognomy, his keen powers of observation of everyday life on the streets (*flâneur par excellence*)[88] all found their reflection in Dostoevsky's later major novels and were transplanted onto the Russian soil in the context of the nineteenth-century Russian philosophical novel.

---

88 Zweig, *Balzac, Dickens, Dostoevsky: Master Builders of the Spirit*, 34.

Chapter Three

The Theme of Money in *Eugénie Grandet* and Dostoevsky's Texts

For Balzac, money was a powerful factor in human behavior, both in his personal life and in the fictional world of his novels. Hyppolite Taine, in his critical study of Balzac, noted that Balzac's financial struggles, which he experienced early on and continued to face throughout his life despite his great success as a writer, strongly influenced all of his works. "He comprehended that money is the great mainspring of modern life. He was accustomed to reckon up the fortunes of his characters, explained their origin, their multiplication; he balanced receipts and expenses and brought into his romances the methods of the counting house. . . . He made business romantic."[1] Balzac himself noted in his earlier treatise *Le Code des gens honnêtes* (1825) that all modern social life is organized around money: "L'argent, par le temps qui court, donne la consideration, les amis, le success, les talents, l'esprit même"[2] (Money, these days, gives consideration, friends, success, talents, and even intelligence).[3] As a self-described "historian of society" (*l'historien des moeurs*),[4] Balzac felt that it was appropriate to study money and its effects on individuals under various circumstances and settings. The novelist Stephan Zweig, analyzing Balzac's creative technique, concurred

---

1   Hippolyte Taine, *Balzac; a Critical Study*, trans. Lorenzo O'Rourke (Folcroft, PA: Folcroft Library Editions, 1973), 90.
2   Maurice Bardèche, *Balzac, Romancier* (Paris: Plon, 1947), 131.
3   Translation mine.
4   Balzac, "L'Avant-propos de la Comédie humaine," 15.

with Taine and many other scholars[5] regarding the importance of money theme for Balzac, noting that Balzac

> investigated money values, and introduced them into his novels. Ever since the days when aristocratic privilege was abolished, ever since the vast differences of status were reduced to a general level of equality, money has come more and more to be the blood and the driving force of social life. Money value gradually came to determine all things; the worth of every passion was estimated in terms of the material sacrifices entailed; every human being was judged by what his income happened to be in hard cash. Money circulates in his novels.[6]

Zweig's observation is especially appropriate for *Eugénie Grandet* where money is the leading force behind Grandet's existence and the most important motive behind all his decisions and actions. Money permeates every emotion in this novel, and even minute details of daily life and house-keeping (coffee with or without sugar? tallow or wax candle? beef broth or chicken broth or perhaps crows' broth?) are intimately connected with money. Grandet's monomaniacal obsession with wealth deeply affects all his relationships, including with the people closest to him—his wife and daughter. Consequently, the tragic fate of the main character, Eugénie, and all the other events in this novel are also predetermined by money.

Balzac's strong association of emotion and passion with money was something that Dostoevsky later actively employed in his own writing. Like Balzac's, Dostoevsky's personal life was greatly influenced by money struggles from the very beginning of his career, filled with debts, creditors, and promissory notes, regular visits to pawnshops, and even a gambling addiction. All of this turmoil found its reflection in his writing. As in Balzac's novels, in Dostoevsky's most important works money is treated as almost one of the principal characters. In *Crime and Punishment*, *The Idiot*, *The Gambler*, *The Raw Youth*, *The Brothers Karamazov*, and many other novels, money functions as a litmus test for characters' integrity and as a plot impetus.

---

5 See Bardèche, *Balzac, Romancier*; Raymond Giraud, *The Unheroic Hero in the Novels of Stendjal, Balzac, and Flaubert* (Whitefish, MT: Literary Licencing LLC, 2011); André Maurois, *Prometheus, The Life of Balzac* (London: Penguin, 1971); and Armine Mortimer, *For Love or for Money: Balzac's Rhetorical Realism* (Columbus, OH: Ohio State University Press, 2011).

6 Zweig, *Balzac, Dickens, Dostoevsky: Master Builders of the Spirit*, 46.

This chapter analyzes the theme of money and avarice in *Eugénie Grandet* and in Dostoevsky's translation. It also traces the textual echoes of the theme of money from *Eugénie Grandet* to Dostoevsky's subsequent works.

Like Dostoevsky, who often based the plots of his novels and stories on the documented events from criminal chronicles that he read in the newspapers, Balzac frequently found his character types in his own environment. Balzac's biographers agree[7] on his tremendous powers of observation that he successfully applied to recreating the rich and vivid environment of *La Comédie humaine.* He himself acknowledged his ability in a letter to Madame Hanska in 1833: "J'ai été pourvu d'une grande puissance d'observation, parce que j'ai été jeté à travers toutes sortes de professions, involontairement"[8] (I had, however, a great power of observation because I was thrown through all kinds of professions, albeit involuntarily).[9]

It is known that at the period between 1830 and 1832 Balzac spent some time near Saumur in Minerolle.[10] Discussing *Eugénie Grandet* in his study *Balzac, Romancier*, Maurice Bardèche mentions that some biographers indicate that among the possible prototypes of Grandet was Monsieur Nivelleau (1767–1847),[11] whom Balzac could have known in Saumur. Monsieur Nivelleau, whose profession is described in the archival records as "négociant commissionnaire faisant les opérations de banque," occupied one of the old bourgeois houses in the older central part of Saumur, rue du Petit-Maure, had an immense fortune, many properties, and was the father to one daughter who later married. In 1822, he acquired a *château* called Montreil-Bellay, and Grandet's purchase of Froidfond is viewed by some biographers as a parallel to that.[12] After Monsieur Nivelleau died, he left a fortune estimated to be greater than two millions francs. But unlike Grandet, Monsieur Nivelleau was not known to have an extremely thrifty lifestyle; on the contrary, his house and the upbringing that he gave to his daughter point to a comfortable lifestyle of the wealthy bourgeoisie of that period, so his figure can be connected to Balzac's character only tangentially.

---

7   See Zweig, *Balzac*, trans. William and Dorothy Rose (New York: Viking Press, 1946); Bardèche. *Balzac, Romancier*; Maurois, *Prometheus*.
8   Honoré de Balzac, *Lettres à l'étrangère*, ed. Saint-John Perse and Mauricette Berne (Paris: Gallimard, 1987), 13.
9   Translation mine.
10 Bardèche, *Balzac, Romancier*, 462.
11 For more see Bardèche, *Balzac, Romancier*, 462.
12 Ibid., 462.

When Balzac first introduces Grandet to the reader, he is presented as an extraordinary character. His first name—Felix—conveys the notion of success and luck,[13] and his last name—Grandet—is connected to the French adjective *grand* (great). The connotation of *grandeur* can be interpreted as having a double significance. On the one hand, Grandet is a "great" man in the sense that he is far more intelligent and capable than other residents of Saumur, and they acknowledge his superiority when they gauge their estimation of future harvest and even their expectations of the weather by watching and interpreting his behavior. On the other hand, he is described as "great" because he has a "grand" ruling passion—a monomaniac obsession with money.

In the beginning of the novel, in the scenes that serve as an exposition to the story, Balzac provides a detailed account of Grandet's fortune building, indicating exact monetary amounts that Grandet started with—two thousand golden louis, the sum that came from his wife's dowry. Over the years Grandet's career as a cooper and prosperous vineyard-owner flourished. A shrewd businessman, he was able to make his fortune partly through profitable deals of supplying local white wine to the Republican armies and partly through deftly buying more vineyards. As time went by, so grew his fortune and influence in town. At one point he even served as mayor of Saumur.

At the time of the first events in the novel, the residents of Saumur do not know the exact amount of his wealth. They simply say that Grandet himself does not know how much money he has: "Monsier, nous avons ici deux or trois maisons millionnaires, mais quant à M.Grandet, il ne connaît pas lui-même sa fortune"[14] (Sir, we have two or three millionaire establishments here; but as for Mr.Grandet, he does not even know himself how rich he is!).[15] At the same time, despite his proverbial richness, Grandet continues to maintain an extremely thrifty and simple lifestyle: his family house is very old and it needs repairs, his clothes are simple, always the same and long out of fashion. His wife and the only daughter Eugénie, his sole heiress, also are forced to share his frugality: they only employ one servant, never go out except to Sunday mass, and make their own clothes and household linens.

---

13   "Felix," Behind the Name, https://www.behindthename.com/name/felix.
14   Balzac, *Eugénie Grandet*, 40.
15   Idem, *Père Goriot, and Eugénie Grandet*, 300.

When Grandet's fortune is first mentioned in the novel, the readers learn about it from the perception of other inhabitants of Saumur:

> Bref, il n'y avait dans Saumur personne qui ne fût persuadé que Monsieur Grandet n'eût un trésor particulier, une cachette pleine de louis, et ne se donnât nuitamment les ineffables jouissances que procure la vue d'une grande masse d'or. Les avaricieux en avaient une sorte de certitude, en voyant les yeux du bonhomme auxquels le métal jaune semblait avoir communiqué ses teintes. Le regard d'un homme accoutumé à tirer de ses capitaux un intérêt aussi énorme, contract nécessairement, comme celui du voluptueux, du joueur ou du courtisan, certaines habitudes indéfinissables, des mouvements furtifs, avides, qui n'échappent point à ses co-religionnaires: ce langage secret forme en quelque sort la francmaçonnerie des passions.[16]

> (Everybody in Saumur was firmly convinced that Monsieur Grandet had a private treasure, a hiding place packed with louis, and that he indulged nightly in the ineffable joys afforded by the sight of great masses of gold. The miserly were practically certain of it whenever they looked at the old man's eyes, which seemed to have absorbed the color of the yellow metal itself. The countenance of a man accustomed to drawing enormous interest on his capital, like that of the voluptuary, the gambler, or the sycophant, acquires of necessity certain indefinable characteristics, certain furtive, greedy, mysterious expressions, always quite obvious to the initiated. This secret language is a kind of free masonry of the passions.)[17]

This brief paragraph gives a very insightful characteristic of Grandet's personality, his psychological motivations, and his attitude towards money. Everything in his movements and the expression of his eyes indicates his belonging to the inner circle of those who are ruled by a single passion, along with the misers: the gamblers, the sensualists, the courtesans. Even his graying hair looks like "silver and gold,"[18] according to his neighbors, and his eyes have acquired the reflection of gold. The peculiar expression of his gaze is indicative of belonging to the league of those to whom Balzac referred to as *francmaçonnerie des passions*.

One should note that at this point in the novel, the narrator only communicates to his readers what others are saying about Grandet, and not

---

16   Idem, *Eugénie Grandet*, 38.
17   Idem, *Père Goriot, and Eugénie Grandet*, 299.
18   Ibid., 303.

his own perception. It is a mediated first impression. Later Dostoevsky would use the same device in *The Brothers Karamazov* introducing Fyodor Karamazov first through the words of those who knew him. Several times in his own novels, Dostoevsky returned to the study of the extreme psychological types ruled by monomaniacal passion, mentioned in this paragraph—the gamblers and the sensualists. For example, in *The Gambler* (1866) the protagonist, Alexei Ivanovich, has a dangerous passion for cards, in *Crime and Punishment* (1866) Svidrigailov is a sinister pleasure-seeker, and in *The Brothers Karamazov* (1880) Dostoevsky created a portrait of an aging voluptuary in Fyodor Karamazov.

Dostoevsky translated the above passage by Balzac in the following manner:

> Словом, в Сомюре не было никого, кто бы не был твердо уверен, что у Гранде спрятан где-нибудь клад, сундучок с червонцами, и что старик по ночам предается невыразимым наслаждениям, доставляемым созерцанием огромной груды золота. Скупые особенно готовы были присягнуть в этом, изучив взгляд старика, взгляд, горевший каким-то отблеском заветного металла. Взор человека, привыкшего смотреть на золото, наслаждаться им, блестит каким-то неопределенным тайным выражением, схватывает неизвестные оттенки, усваивает необъяснимые привычки, как взгляд развратника, игрока или придворного; взор этот быстр и робок, жаден, таинствен; обычные его знают, научились ему: это—условный знак, франкмасонство страсти.[19]

> (In short, there was no one in Saumur who was not sure that Grandet hid a treasure, a chest of *chervontsy*, somewhere, and that the old man at night surrendered to the unspeakable pleasures provided by the contemplation of a huge pile of gold. Misers were especially ready to swear by this, having studied the old man's gaze, a glance burning with some reflection of the treasured metal. The look of a man accustomed to look at gold, enjoy it, glitters with an indefinite secret expression, grasps unknown shades, assimilates unexplained habits, like the eyes of a debauchee, gambler or courtier; This look is quick and timid, greedy, mysterious; the accustomed to it know it, have mastered it: this is a conventional sign, freemasonry of passion.)[20]

---

19 Dostoevskii, *Evgeniia Grande*, 12.
20 Translation mine.

Dostoevsky's translation of this passage is important on several levels. First, there are several notable substitutions: French louis are replaced with the Russian word describing any foreign gold coins (*chervontsy*), to make the text easier to understand for an ordinary Russian reader.[21] Dostoevsky also provides Grandet with a little chest (*сундучок*) where he supposedly keeps his gold. This word, used in diminutive form, evokes Russian fairy tales, and links it to Russian literary tradition, specifically to Alexander Pushkin's short tragedy *The Miserly Knight* (*Скупой рыцарь*) written in 1830. The context of Pushkin's tragedy, and the echo of the old miser from that play, can be felt in Dostoevsky's treatment of the Old Grandet.

Dostoevsky's Portrayal of Grandet and Pushkin's The Miserly Knight (1830)

As noted by Jorge Luis Borges in his essay on multiple translations of *A Thousand and One Night*, literary translations are always embedded in the context of a target literary system. For Russian literary tradition, Pushkin's literary legacy is paramount, and the echoes and allusions to Pushkin's texts can be found in a great number of canonical works of the nineteenth and twentieth centuries. It has been noted[22] that Pushkin's works were also very important for Dostoevsky from his early childhood to his death. He considered Pushkin to be the greatest Russian poet and kept reading his poetry and prose all his life. Pushkin's small tragedy *The Miserly Knight* (or *The Covetous Knight*) was very familiar to young Dostoevsky. In this short play, the plot revolves around a conflict between a rich old miserly father and his irresponsible son, who begs him for money unsuccessfully. The rich old man eventually dies without reconciliation with his son, but he worries about the fate of his fortune that may be squandered by his heir, and his last thoughts and words are addressed to his treasure that he keeps in locked chests: "Where are the keys? My keys!" ("Где ключи? Ключи, ключи мои!")[23]

The second scene of Pushkin's play where the miserly knight goes to his cellar alone to look at his treasure chests is especially relevant to our discussion. Very similar to Dostoevsky in his translation, Pushkin uses

---

21 For more on this translation strategy see Venuti, *The Translation Studies Reader*, 55–56.
22 Leonid Grossman, *Dostoevskii* (Moscow, Russia: Molodaia gvardiia, 1965), 20–22, 27.
23 Aleksandr Pushkin, "Skupoi rytsar'," in his *Polnoe sobranie sochinenii* (Moscow, Russia: Voskresenie, 1995), vol. 7, 121.

the metaphor of anticipating sensual pleasure and compares a miser to an ardent lover waiting for an amorous *rendez-vous*:

> Как молодой повеса ждет свиданья
>
> С какой-нибудь развратницей лукавой
>
> Иль дурой, им обманутой, так я
>
> Весь день минуты ждал, когда сойду
>
> В подвал мой тайный, к верным сундукам.
>
> Счастливый день! Могу сегодня я
>
> В шестой сундук (в сундук еще неполный)
>
> Гость золота накопленного всыпать.
>
> Не много кажется, но понемногу
>
> Сокровища растут.[24]

> (As full of hot impatience as a rake
>
> Before a meeting with an artful temptress
>
> Or artless maid caught in his web of lies,
>
> So did I wait all day for that sweet moment
>
> When I could visit this my secret cache
>
> And faithful chests. O blessed day! For I
>
> Into my sixth, as yet but half-filled chest,
>
> Can put today this gold that I have hoarded—
>
> The merest handful, true, but treasures grow
>
> Little by little.)[25]

Pushkin's miserly baron experiences the whole range of human emotions while contemplating his gold. In his monologue, in the second scene among his chests, he says as he opens the chests and admires his splendid shiny coins, that he feels absolute power and imagines himself a ruler of the world. This nightly ritual is a pinnacle of his existence. Pushkin's character has renounced all human connections, even love, in favor of his sole passion—accumulating more gold. His exalted emotional state while contemplating his chests filled with gold is very close to the image that Dostoevsky creates in his translation of the passage describing Grandet's nightly vigils in his study where he goes to examine his riches.

---

24 Ibid., 110.

25 Alexander Pushkin, *The Covetous Knight*, trans. Irina Zheleznova, http://ocls.kyivlibs. org.ua/pushkin/perekladi_1/Pushkin_english/The_Covetous_Knight/The_Covetous_Knight.htm.

Хочу себе сегодня пир устроить:
Зажгу свечу пред каждым сундуком,
И все их отопру, и стану сам
Средь них глядеть на блещущие груды.

(Зажигает свечи и отпирает сундуки один за другим)

Я царствую! . . Какой волшебный блеск!
Послушна мне, сильна моя держава;
В ней счастие, в ней честь моя и слава!
Я царствую. . . .[26]

(Today I wish to hold a fête, for so
My fancy bids me do. The chests unlocking,
Beside each one I'll set a lighted candle
And revel in the sight of so much splendour.

Lights candles and unlocks the chests one after another.

What magic brilliance! I'm a prince, I reign
Over a proud and mighty realm; my fame
And happiness and honour rest upon it!
Today I am a prince, I reign. . . .)[27]

In this scene in Pushkin's poem money is portrayed as the symbol of supreme power and control over the world, and for that reason for the miserly baron all human pleasures are surpassed by the pleasure of owning the gold. Contemplating the gold is almost a religious ritual for him, as he lights a candle in front of each of his chests. Gold here functions not only as a physical representation of wealth, but rather it becomes a transcendent symbol of omnipotence, a Holy Grail, in the eyes of the character as he contemplates his treasures.

While Pushkin's poem is set in a medieval castle and his miser has six large chests to fit the grandeur of the setting, Dostoevsky adjusts his setting to a more modest scale. In his translation Grandet only has one small chest (*сундучок*). One should note the use of the diminutive form of the word for "chest." Diminutives in Russian usually convey the speaker's affection and

---

26 Pushkin, "Skupoi rytsar'," 121.
27 Pushkin, *The Covetous Knight.*

love for the item, animate or inanimate, and they can also indicate an intimate relationship and familiar closeness. For example, parents use diminutives routinely when talking to their children, lovers use diminutives when calling each other by their first names, and so forth. In addition to "little chest," *сундучок* in this initial scene, Dostoevsky often uses the diminutive form for the Russian word for "money"—*денежки*—to describe Grandet's treasure throughout the novel. This usage conveys to the Russian readers Grandet's deep affection for money and his intimate knowledge of it.

Grandet, like Pushkin's miserly baron from *The Covetous Knight*, likes to examine, touch, and admire his gold coins at night in complete solitude. He has a study behind a heavy closed door where no one is allowed to come in and he works alone there every night. Balzac even compares Grandet's study to the furnace of alchemist or a laboratory to sustain the metaphor of the mystery of gold production:

> Personne, pas même madame Grandet, n'avait la permission d'y venir. L'avare voulait rester seul comme un alchimiste à son fourneau. Là, sans doute, quelque cachette avait été très habilement pratiquées; là, se faisaient nuitamment et en secret les calculs de manière à ce que les gens d'affaires, voyant toujours M. Grandet prêt à tout, pouvaient imaginer qu'il avait à ses ordres une fée ou un démon. Là, sans doute, quand Nanon ronflait à ébranler les planchers, quand le chien-loup veillait et bâillait dans la cour, quand madame et mademoiselle Grandet étaient bien endormies, venait le vieux tonnelier choyer, caresser, couver, cuver, cercler son or. Les murs étaient épais, les contrevents discrets. Lui seul avait la clé de ce laboratoire, où, dit-on, il consultait des plans sur lequels ses arbres à fruits étaient désignés et où il chiffrait ses produits à un provin, à une bourrée près.[28]

> (Nobody, not even madame Grandet, was allowed to enter; the old man preferred to be alone there like an alchemist at his furnace. There, doubtless, some hiding-place had been very skillfully contrived; there were stored the titles to his estates; there hung the scales for weighing his gold coins; there every night and in secret he made out his receipts, vouchers, and estimates, so that the business men, who always found Grandet with everything in readiness, could imagine that he had a fairy or a demon at his command. There, doubtless, while Nanon snored till the rafters shook, while the wolf-dog kept watch and yawned in the courtyard, while Madame and

---

28 Balzac, *Eugénie Grandet*, 117.

Mademoiselle Grandet were sound asleep, the old cooper came to cherish, caress, gloat over his gold and pack it away in casks. The walls were thick, the shutters discreet. He alone had the key to this laboratory, it was said, he consulted maps on which his fruit trees were marked, and where he figured out his produce to the last twig of vine and almost to the last stick of wood.[29]

In the French text, in addition to the nightly voluptuous ritual of inspecting and admiring the gold, Balzac also shows in the description of Grandet's study the shrewd business aspects of Grandet's personality: his meticulous daily bookkeeping, his careful calculations of expenses, and his thorough knowledge of his properties and their potential for growing vines and projected harvest. When Grandet goes to his office every night, he does not only admire his gold coins there; he also works, writes out receipts, and plans new business ventures. Thus, in Balzac's novel Grandet is not solely a miser fixated on the material possession of gold, but also a cunning businessman who built his fortune on his sharp business instincts and thorough knowledge of his properties.

These aspects of Grandet's character as a successful and adroit businessman are underplayed in Dostoevsky's translation. On the one hand, Pushkin's portrayal of the main character in *The Miserly Knight* serves as the primary reference image for Dostoevsky's description of Old Grandet, and on the other hand, for Dostoevsky as a writer it was the psychological study of avarice that was the most compelling. For these reasons, he chose to amplify the features that focus on Grandet's monomania rather than his business acumen. In Dostoevsky's portrayal, Grandet is a miser *par excellence* driven by his sole passion to accumulate more money and deriving sensual pleasure from possessing and accumulating physical masses of gold. This is how Dostoevsky translated the same passage:

> Никто, не исключая и госпожи Гранде, не смел входить в кабинет старика. Скряга любил уединение, как алхимик любит его подле своего очага. Здесь-то, вероятно, была запрятана заветная кубышка, хранились бумаги и документы, висели весы, на которых Гранде взвешивал свои червонцы; тут-то совершались по ночам все дела и начинания его, сводились счеты, итоги, писались квитанции, векселя; и не диво, что люди, видя, что у Гранде всегда все готово, всегда все поспевает к сроку, и не замечая, когда и где он работает, приписывали

---

29 Idem, *Père Goriot, and Eugénie Grandet*, 344.

это какому-то колдовству, чародейству. Здесь, когда ночью Нанета храпела уже так, что дрожали стены, когда собака бродила по двору, а жена и дочь скряги спали крепким сном, старик раскрывал свою кубышку, пересчитывал свое золото, глядел на него жадно, по целым часам взвешивал его на весах, на руках своих, целовал свое сокровище с любовью, с наслаждением. . . Стены крепки, ставни задвинуты, ключ у него. Старик в тишине своего уединения не ограничивался настоящим, загадывал в будущность, манил грядущие денежки и рассчитывал барыши за плоды, еще не родившиеся и не убранные.[30]

(Nobody, even Mrs. Grandet, dared to enter the old man's office. The miser loved solitude, as an alchemist loves his solitude near his furnace. Here, probably, was his hidden treasure egg, here he stored papers and documents, the scales on which Grandet weighed his *chervontsy*;[31] here, at night, all his deals and undertakings were done, bills, totals, receipts, promissory notes were written; And it is not surprising that people, seeing that Grandet always has everything ready, always ready on time, and not noticing when and where he works, attributed it to some kind of magic or sorcery. Here, at night when Nanette already snored so that the walls trembled as the dog wandered around the yard, and the wife and daughter of the miser were soundly asleep, the old man opened his treasure chest, counted his gold, looked at it greedily, weighed it for hours on the scales, and in his hands; he kissed his treasure with love, with pleasure. . . The walls are strong, the shutters are closed, the key is with him. The old man, in the silence of his seclusion, did not limit himself to the present, he made plans for the future, beckoned for future money, and calculated profits for fruits that were not yet seeded and not harvested.)[32]

In his interpretation of Grandet's character, Dostoevsky repeated the word "miser," *скряга*, three times on this page alone, and many more times throughout the novel in order to emphasize cupidity as Grandet's over-whelming mania. This repetition further links Dostoevsky's translation to Pushkin's text. By contrast, Balzac was very conscious of Grandet's potential connection to Harpagon in Moliere's *L'Avare* in the eyes of French readers, and he made a lot of effort in his work on the depiction of Old Grandet to distance his complex character from this earlier reference point. As

---

30 Dostoevskii, *Evgeniia Grande*, 60.
31 Foreign gold coins.
32 Translation mine.

Pierre-Georges Castex noted in his commentaries to Balzac's text,[33] while working on multiple revisions of the novel Balzac tried to avoid referring to Grandet as a miser, as he felt that it would oversimplify and reduce Grandet's personality to a single trait. Instead Balzac calls Grandet in various junctures of the novel *bonhomme* (good man), *tonnelier* (barrel-maker), *le père Grandet* (father Grandet). These characteristics highlight multiple sides of Grandet's character: he has the respect of his neighbours (good man), he is a father who cares about his daughter, and he is also a successful barrel-maker. These traits give more complexity, depth, nuance, and interest to his larger-than-life character.

In his translation, Dostoevsky brings into the foreground Grandet's ability to derive sensual pleasure from admiring his gold, adding the sentence that is not in the original: "the miser . . . kissed his treasure with love, with pleasure." Dostoevsky also highlights the magic or alchemy behind Grandet's financial success by saying that Grandet in his solitary evening hours in his study was "atttracting his future money"—манил грядущие денежки. This sentence is also absent from Balzac's text. The verb манить—"to draw, to lure, to entice"—in Russian is associated with sorcery, and a phenomenal ability of attracting something or someone. Thus, while Balzac's description of Grandet's nightly activities in his study talks about his daily habits of meticulous bookkeeping, his preparedness for new deals, and his general business acumen (he consulted maps on which his fruit trees were marked, and where he figured out his produce to the last twig of vine and almost to the last stick of wood), Dostoevsky's portrayal of Grandet focuses instead on his singular sensual obsession with gold and attributes his wealth to his uncanny ability to "attract" money. One also notices that in this passage Dostoevsky used the diminutive form of Russian word for money—денежки—in keeping his stylistic choice for diminutives throughout the novel. This word highlights Grandet's lovingly intimate relationship with money.

There is also a significant textual parallel between the beginning of the novel and the finale. Introducing Grandet in the opening pages, Balzac uses the verb *communiquer* as he describes the eyes of Grandet to which the gold seemed to transfer its color ("les yeux auxquels le métal jaune semblait avoir communiqué ses teintes").[34] This verb is repeated on the final page

33 Balzac, *Eugénie Grandet*, comment. Pierre-George Castex (Paris, France: Garnier, 1965), 284–285.

34 Balzac, *Eugénie Grandet*, 38.

of the novel, when Balzac describes the mature Eugénie and the changes in her personality. While she is very generous with her charitable contributions, she begins to resemble her father in certain ways: she maintains the same extremely simple and frugal lifestyle for herself, uses his expression *Nous verrons cela* ("we shall see"), and even adheres to the custom of not starting to light the fireplace before November, just as Grandet himself used to do. As Balzac describes the mature Eugénie, he writes that her heart grew cold because money had to transfer its cold colors to her heavenly life ("L'argent devait communiquer ses teintes froides a cette vie celeste").[35] Thus, the family connection between the father and the daughter is also reflected in the language.

In Dostoevsky's translation, this exact repetition of the verb is absent because he deliberately chooses not to emphasize the resemblance between the father and the daughter. So, when Dostoevsky describes Grandet's eyes in the beginning of the novel, he says instead that they "were burning with the reflection of the cherished metal." When he talks about Evgenia in the end, he paraphrases and intensifies Balzac's original, saying that "Деньги должны были сообщить свои холодные оттенки этой небесной жизни и внушить недоверие к чувствам женщине, которая вся была чувство!"[36] (Money had to shed on its cold shadows to this celestial life and implant a distrust to feelings of the heart in this woman who was all feeling). Talking about Grandet in the beginning of the novel, Dostoevsky emphasizes his obsession with gold, and since there is a cliché of saying that someone's eyes are "burning with passion," he makes Grandet's eyes gleam with reflection of gold, expanding the metaphor and tying it to Grandet's manic avarice.

Dostoevsky also added an epithet *заветный* (cherished) for the reflection of gold in Grandet's eyes, replacing Balzac's clichéd reference to gold as "yellow metal"—*le métal jaune*—with "cherished metal"—*заветный металл*. The Russian adjective *заветный* is significant, and its usage is associated with such phrases as "cherished dreams," "cherished hopes," "cherished secrets"—*заветные мечты, заветные надежды, заветные тайны*. By attributing this epithet to gold, Dostoevsky's translation again brings to the foreground Grandet's love for money and his humanization and personification of it.

---

35 Ibid., 381.
36 Dostoevskii, *Evgeniia Grande*, 225.

Evgenia's Treasure and Dostoevsky's Mr. Prokharchin (1846)

The stark contrast between outwardly displayed poverty and hidden fortune that is never enjoyed was something that Dostoevsky found intriguing from a psychological viewpoint. He returned to this theme of hidden wealth and cupidity in his own short story *Mr. Prokharchin* written shortly after he finished translating *Eugénie Grandet*. This short story was published in 1846 in *Otechestvennye zapiski* (Notes of fatherland), one of the leading Russian literary journals in Saint Petersburg.

In this story, the theme of avarice is given an ironic treatment, and several details from *Eugénie Grandet* reappear here in a parodic form. Dostoevsky transplants elements of Balzac's novels to Saint Petersburg: there is a shabby boarding house run by an eccentric middle-aged landlady and filled with a dozen peculiar tenants in various life situations. Among them resides an extremely miserly Mr. Prokharchin, who has been renting a room at that boarding house for many years. Like Grandet, he is obsessed with a single secret passion: his life-long goal is accumulating wealth.

But while Balzac's central character is a very strong and powerful person, whose will and intelligence tower over his peers, Dostoevsky's attention in his story is focused on the plight of "a little man"—*маленький человек*. Thus, Dostoevsky's Mr. Prokharchin is an ordinary man, leading the unremarkable existence of a poor clerk in a big office somewhere in Saint Petersburg. The only distinguishing feature of Mr. Prokharchin is his extreme avarice. Mr. Prokharchin, similarly to Pushkin's miserly knight and Balzac's Grandet, views money not as the means to an end, but as an end itself. He does not have any plans to spend it or to alter his lifestyle once he accumulates a certain amount. Unlike Pushkin's or Balzac's characters, however, Dostoevsky's Mr. Prokharchin is created as a parody of extreme cupidity, so that his story contains many comedic elements. For example, Mr. Prokharchin is so extremely frugal that he even does not drink tea and chooses instead a strange herbal brew because it costs less.

If Grandet's last name implies greatness, Mr. Prokharchin's last name is derived from Russian word *харчи* referring to a type of meat-based soup, or more generally, any food. It is worth noting that etymology of this Russian word is connected to the Arabic word *xardž* meaning "household expenses."[37] Thus, the last name of Dostoevsky's character consists of the

---

37 Maks Fassmer, *Etimologicheskii slovar' russkogo iazyka*, trans. O. N. Trubachev, ed. B. A. Larin (Moscow, Russia: Progress, 1986).

prefix *pro-* (about) and the root *-kharch-* (soup), creating from a stylistic point of view a very low-range surname literally meaning "Mr. Aboutsoup."

Any additional details that Dostoevsky chooses to include about Prokharchin's lifestyle serve the same purpose of highlighting the comic elements. For example, at one point Dostoevsky mentions that Mr. Prokharchin does not wear any undergarments so that he can save on doing laundry: "all the days of his life on earth he was a stranger to socks, hand-kerchiefs, and all such things."[38] And when Mr. Prokharchin unexpectedly dies, he is buried in his nicest and only suit.

Dostoevsky mentions that the only valuable item that Mr. Prokharchin has in his possession a treasure chest—*сундучок*—with an excellent German lock. It is exactly the same word that Dostoevsky used to describe Grandet's hidden treasure. Similarly to the residents of Saumur, some of the tenants of the boarding house long suspect that Mr. Prokharchin has diligently saved all his earnings and keeps the money in his treasure chest under lock and key. When Mr. Prokharchin dies, the tenants discover by an ironic turn of events in the story that his treasure chest only had some old clothes. However, they find by chance that his old mattress has a fresh hole cut out with a knife, and suddenly from this hole an avalanche of gold coins of various denominations rolls out. All the coins are neatly wrapped in paper to protect the gold and treated almost like art objects. Very long and detailed enumerations of silver and gold coins of various denominations and origin echo the description of contents of Eugénie's red purse when she counts her money before giving it to Charles, but this avalanche of coins again is depicted as a parody, and the discovered sum is much smaller.

> Благородные целковики, солидные, крепкие полуторарублевики, хорошенькая монета полтинник, плебеи четвертачки, двугривеннички, даже малообещающая, старушечья мелюзга, гривенники и пятаки серебром,—всё в особых бумажках, в самом методическом и солидном порядке. Были и редкости: два какие-то жетона, один наполеондор, одна неизвестно какая, но только очень редкая монетка . . . Некоторые из рубликов относились тоже к глубокой древности; истертые и изрубленные елизаветинские, немецкие крестовики, петровские монеты, екатерининские; были, например, теперь весьма редкие монетки, старые пятиалтыннички, проколотые для ношения в ушах,

---

38 Fyodor Dostoyevsky, "Mr. Prokharchin," trans. Constance Garnett, https://www.gutenberg.org/ebooks/36034.

все совершенно истертые, но с законным количеством точек; даже медь была, но вся уже зеленая, ржавая . . . Нашли одну красную бумажку—но более не было. Наконец, когда кончилась вся анатомия и, неоднократно встряхнув тюфячий чехол, нашли, что ничего не гремит, сложили все деньги на стол и принялись считать. С первого взгляда можно было даже совсем обмануться и смекнуть прямо на миллион—такая была огромная куча! Но миллиона не было, хотя и вышла, впрочем, сумма чрезвычайно значительная—ровно две тысячи четыреста девяносто семь рублей с полтиною.[39]

(Noble silver roubles, stout solid rouble and a half pieces, pretty half rouble coins, plebeian quarter roubles, twenty kopeck pieces, even the unpromising old crone's small fry of ten and five kopeck silver pieces—all done up in separate bits of paper in the most methodical and systematic way; there were curiosities also, two counters of some sort, one napoléon d'or, one very rare coin of some unknown kind . . . Some of the roubles were of the greatest antiquity, they were rubbed and hacked coins of Elizabeth, German kreutzers, coins of Peter, of Catherine; there were, for instance, old fifteen-kopeck pieces, now very rare, pierced for wearing as earrings, all much worn, yet with the requisite number of dots; there was even copper, but all of that was green and tarnished . . . They found one red note, but no more. At last, when the dissection was quite over and the mattress case had been shaken more than once without a clink, they piled all the money on the table and set to work to count it. At the first glance one might well have been deceived and have estimated it at a million, it was such an immense heap. But it was not a million, though it did turn out to be a very considerable sum—exactly 2497 roubles and a half.)[40]

Dostoevsky's depiction in *Mr. Prokharchin* of gold, silver, and copper coins pouring out from the mattress with a notable absence of any paper money except for "one red bill" also echoes the description of Grandet's gold collection. Moreover, this episode is connected to Balzac's novel not only at the direct textual level, but at the interpretive level of describing the psychology of avarice. In this story of hidden fortune under the guise of extreme poverty, one can see the depth of human obsession with gold that becomes a psychological deviation. For Mr. Prokharchin, similar to

39 Dostoevskii, *Polnoe sobraniie sochinenii i pisem* (Saint Petersburg, Russia: Nauka, 2013), I:298.
40 Dostoyevsky, "Mr. Prokharchin."

Old Grandet, as Dostoevsky saw this character, money is the physical representation of happiness and security, and the only thing that he can control in his miserable life. After Prokharchin's death other tenants wonder why he did not put his money into the bank but chose to keep it in his old decaying mattress. One of them says that Mr. Prokharchin was not intelligent enough. However, the story suggests that Mr. Prokharchin actually liked being physically close to his fortune and derived emotional comfort, security, and reassurance in its proximity. Similarly, when Old Grandet is paralyzed and about to die, he chooses to sit facing his gold, and says that the sight of it "warms him up." The physical presence of gold replaces for Grandet the human warmth that has been lost in his relationship with his daughter and wife. This will be discussed in greater detail later in the chapter, as we look at the translation of the final scenes of Grandet's life.

The pleasure Grandet derives from admiring his coins is manifold. A large part of it is sensual: Balzac even uses the noun associated with sexual pleasure, as he writes that Grandet "indulged nightly in the ineffable joys"—*les ineffables jouissances*. Grandet feels the same pleasure when he inspects biannually Eugénie's "marriage dozen"—the collection of gold coins that he has been giving her over the years as his gifts for her birthday and New Year's Day that would become part of her dowry.

The theme of "the marriage dozen" becomes a leitmotif for the events in the novel. First, it is something that connects Old Grandet and Eugénie, as he thinks about her future as a bride. Later, when she gives the money from her "marriage dozen" to Charles, it functions as a transference of love that she felt previously for her father to another man whom she hopes to marry. When Old Grandet finds out about her action, he sees it as a betrayal of his hopes for her and his affection, and he curses Eugénie, vowing to disinherit her and severing all family ties with her. Seven years later, when Old Grandet has already died, Charles returns to Paris having rebuilt his fortune in the West Indies and is about to marry rich Mademoiselle d'Aubrion. He sends Eugénie a check for eight thousand francs, which includes the amount that she gave him plus interest. Thus, her "marriage dozen" is symbolically returned to her with his promise of marriage, and it completes the circle that this money has made in the novel.

In his description of the "marriage dozen" Balzac focuses the readers' attention on the contents of Eugénie's purse and gives a long account of her precious coin collection:

Elle sépara d'abord vent portugaises encore neuves, frappées sous le règne de Jean V, en 1725, valant reéllement au change cinq lisbonines ou chacune cent soixante-huit francs soixante quatre centimes, lui disait son père, mais dont la valeur conventionelle était de 180 fr., attendu la rareté, la beauté desdites pièces, qui reluisaient comme des soleils.

Item, cinq génovines ou pièces de cent livres de Gènes, autre monnaie rare et valant quatre-vingt-sept francs au change, mais cent francs pour les amateurs d'or. Elles lui venaient du vieux monsieur La Bertillière.

Item, trois quadruples d'or espagnols de Philippe V, frappés en 1729, donnés par madame Gentillet, qui, en lui les offrant, lui disait toujours la même phrase: "Ce cher serin-là, ce petit jaunet, vaut quatre-vingt-dix-huit livres! Gardez-le bien, ma mignonne, ce sera la fleur de votre trésor."

Item, ce que son père estimait le plus (l'or de ses pièces était au vingt-trois carats et une fraction), cent ducats de Hollande, fabriqués en l'an 1756, et valant près de douze francs.

Item, une grande curiosité, des espèces de médailles précieuses aux avares, trois roupies au signe de la balance et cinq roupies au signe de la vierge, toutes d'or pure au vingt-quatre carats, la sublime monnaie du grand Mogol, et dont chacune valait trente-sept francs quarante centimes, au poids; mais au moins cinquante francs pour les connaisseurs qui aiment à manier l'or.

Item, le napoléon de quarante francs, reçu l'avant-vieille et q'elle avait négligemment mis dans sa bourse rouge.

Ce trésor contenait de pièces neuves et vierges, de véritables morceaux d'art don't le père Grandet s'informait parfois et qu'il voulait revoir, afin d'en détailler à sa fille les vertus intrinséques, comme la beauté du cordon, la claret du plat, la richesse des lettres dont les vives arêtes n'etaient pas encore rayées. . . . Elle . . . parvint enfin à comprendre, après quelques fautes du calcul, qu'elle possédait environ cinq mille huit cents francs en valeurs réelles, qui, conventionnellement, pouvaient se vendre près de deux mille écus.[41]

(First she took out twenty Portuguese coins, still new, struck in the reign of John V in 1725. At the present rate of exchange they were actually worth five lisbonnines or a hundred and sixty-eight francs sixty-four centimes each, but their conventional value was a hundred and eighty francs on account of the rarity and beauty of the said coins, which shone like the sun. *Item,*

---

41 Balzac, *Eugénie Grandet*, 238–240.

five genovines or hundred-franc pieces from Genoa, another rare coin worth eighty-seven francs on the exchange, but a hundred francs to collectors. She has inherited them from old Monsieur de la Bertellière. *Item*, three gold quadruples, Spanish, of Philip V, struck in 1729, given her by Madame Gentillet, who always repeated the same phrase with each gift: "This dear little canary, this yellow boy, is worth ninety-eight francs! Take good care of him, my darling, he'll be the flower of your treasure." *Item* [these were valued most highly by her father, the gold in them being twenty-three carats and a fraction], a hundred Dutch ducats, struck in the year 1756 and worth nearly thirteen francs each. *Item* [a great curiosity . . . a species of medals almost sacred to misers], three rupees with the sign of the Scales, and five rupees with the sign of the Virgin, all in pure gold of twenty-five carats; the magnificent coins of the Great Mogul, each of which was worth by mere weight thirty-seven francs, forty centimes, but at least fifty francs to those connoisseurs who love to handle gold. *Item*, the napoleon of forty francs received two days before, which she had put carelessly in her red purse.

This treasure consisted of new and virgin coins, real works of art. Old Grandet often asked about them and liked to see them from time to time in order to point out to his daughter their intrinsic merits, such as the beauty of the milled edges, the brightness of the face, the richness of the letters, whose sharp ridges were not yet worn down. . . . She figured out, after making a few mistakes, that she possessed about five thousand eight hundred francs in actual value, which might be sold to collectors for close to six thousand francs.)[42]

This very specific and complex description, rich in historic detail, plays a very important role in the novel. Apart from introducing a multitude of historic coins from various countries into the novel, it sets up a multitiered value system for gold: its actual value (*la valeur réelle*) versus possible projected value (*valeur pour les amateurs*). There is also the added symbolic value of *le douzain de mariage* for Eugénie perceived by her father and her relatives who have been giving her the coins over the years. Another symbolic value is assigned to her money by Eugénie herself who values her treasure only as the means to help Charles. All these meanings are linked to one specific type of object, giving a tangible representation of her fortune. For Balzac's characters, the physical embodiment of wealth in gold, silver,

---

42 Balzac, *Père Goriot, and Eugénie Grandet*, 411–412.

and precious stones signifies solidity and reliability, while paper money, by contrast, is perceived as suspect, ephemeral, and not trustworthy.

For Grandet, a certain concrete value represented by gold coins as opposed to more contemporary paper money reflects his old-time habits and beliefs, and it is connected to his traditional way of doing business through solid investments in land and vines. This traditional old-fashioned pre-capitalist approach to wealth-building is contrasted in the novel with the more recent trends in Parisian society reflecting the nascent capitalist economy—ephemeral fortunes made and lost in various get-rich-quick schemes, as illustrated by Charles who has outwardly all the markings of wealth but in reality owns nothing except debts left after his father's bankruptcy. These rapid changes in nineteenth-century French society from the traditional beliefs of the old bourgeoisie to the emerging new trends of quick enterprises for money-making held a special interest for Balzac as a self-proclaimed *l'historien des moeurs*.[43] Some of the novels of *La Comedie humaine* (*La Maison Nucingen*, *César Birotteau*) explore this subject.

Balzac's detailed description of Eugénie's purse is very challenging to translate since it contains a plethora of names of various historical coins, their design elements, and other specifics, but Dostoevsky was able to render it sucessfully in Russian, even though he did not have a good French dictionary or any other references available to him.[44] His meticulous work on this difficult passage is later echoed in his long enumeration of various coin denominations in Mr. Prokharchin's mattress.

This is how Dostoevsky translated the same passage, again making several changes to the original that will be discussed below:

> Сперва отделила она двадцать португальских червонцев, вычеканенных еще при Иоанне V, в 1725 году. Они стоили по действительному курсу не менее пяти лиссабонских червонцев, или по крайней мере сто шестьдесят восемь франков шестьдесят четыре сантима каждый, как ценил их старик отец. Но настоящая цена их была в сто восемьдесят франков, по красоте и редкости монеты, сияющей подобно солнцу. Потом пять генуэзских червонцев, ходивших по сто ливров в Генуе, стоивших на обмен восемьдесят семь франков каждый; но для любителей монета ценилась и в сто франков. Они достались Евгении от покойного старичка Ла Бертельера. Далее, три золотых испанских

---

43   Balzac, "L'Avant-propos de la Comédie humaine," 15.

44   Dostoevskii, *Evgeniia Grande*, 238.

кадрюпля времен Филиппа V, вычеканенных в 1729 году,—подарок г-жи Жантильи, которая каждый раз, даря их, говорила:—Этот хорошенький червончик, этот желтенький милушка стоит девяносто восемь ливров. Береги, душенька, это—красавчик в твоем сокровище.

Затем, и что наиболее нравилось старику Гранде (потому что золота было в каждой монете двадцать три карата), сто голландских червонцев, вычеканенных в 1756 году и ходивших по тринадцати франков.

Далее, собрание медалей и редкой монеты, драгоценное для нумизматиков и скупых: три рупии со знаками Весов и пять рупий со знаками Девы, цельные, чистого золота, в двадцать четыре карата, великолепные денежные знаки Великого Могола, каждый из них стоил тридцать семь франков сорок сантимов по весу, но для охотников не менее пятидесяти франков.

Наконец, наполеондор стоимостью сорок франков, полученный третьего дня от отца и небрежно брошенный Евгенией в красный кошелек.

Сокровище это состояло из монет чистеньких, светленьких, настоящих художественных изделий; старик Гранде часто любовался ими, часто засматривался на них и по целым часам толковал дочери о красоте их, изъяснял ей их редкость, чистоту обреза, блеск поля, изящество букв, еще свежих, блистающих, не изглаженных временем. ... После нескольких ошибок в счете она наконец добралась до итога: всего было около пяти тысяч восьмисот франков по ходячей цене, или, на охотника, около двух тысяч экю.[45]

(First, she separated twenty Portuguese gold coins [*chervontsy*], minted under John V, in 1725. They were worth at the current exchange rate at least five Lisbon chervontsi, or at least one hundred and sixty-eight francs sixty-four centimes each, as her old father valued them. But the real price was one hundred and eighty francs, for the beauty and rarity of the coin, shining like the sun. Then five Genoese *chervontsy*, which were worth about a hundred livres in Genoa, were exchanging at eighty-seven francs each; but for fans of the coin they were valued a hundred francs. They came to Eugenia from the late old Le Bertellier. Further, the three gold Spanish doublons of the time of Philip V, minted in 1729, are the gift of Mme. Gentillet, who each time

---

45 Dostoevskii, *Evgeniia Grande*, 133–134.

giving them, said: "This pretty little *chervonchik*, this yellow-faced beauty, is worth ninety-eight livres. Take care of it, darling, this is the handsome one in your treasure."

Then, and that was what the Old Grandet liked the most [because there was twenty-three carats of gold in every coin], one hundred Dutch *chervontsy*, minted in 1756 and each worth thirteen francs.

Next, a collection of medals and rare coins, precious to numismatists and misers: three rupees with Libra signs and five rupees with Virgo signs, each piece containing twenty-four carats of pure gold, magnificent Mogul money, each worth thirty-seven francs forty centimes by weight, but for collectors not less than fifty francs.

Finally, a Napoleon worth forty francs, received the other day from her father and carelessly thrown by Eugenia into her red purse.

The treasure consisted of clean, light coins, real art objects; Old Grandet often admired them, often looked at them and for hours he described their beauty to his daughter, explained to her their rarity, the crispness of the edges, the brilliance of the field, the elegance of the letters, still fresh, glistening, not dulled by the time. . . . After a few errors in count, she finally got the final result: there were about five thousand eight hundred francs at the current price, or, for an amateur, about two thousand crowns.)

Dostoevsky made some alterations to this complex description, such as referring to Eugénie's gold coins as *chervontsy* to make the passage easier to read for his Russian audience who at that time was used to calling all foreign gold coins by this name.[46] Originally, *chervontsy* referred to old Russian gold coins because they were made from higher grade of pure gold having a reddish tint (old Proto-Slavic root *čьrvjenъ* means "red").[47] Dostoevsky also added many diminutives to the words of Aunt Gentillet as she talks to her niece about the gold. In Dostoevsky's translation, Aunt Gentillet talks about her coins using epithets that are usually applied to people: *хорошенький червончик* (two diminutives here, "little cute gold coin"), *желтенький милушка* (two diminutives again, "little yellow darling"), *красавчик* (again, a dimunitive: "little handsome boy"). Using the diminutive forms that convey warmth and affection in the context of money indicates a chasm between the rest of the world where these words are reserved

---

46 V. Borodulin, ed., *Illiustrirovannyi entsiklopedicheskii slovar'* (Moscow, Russia: Autopan, 1998), https://illustrated_dictionary.academic.ru/13056/Червонец.

47 "Chervonets," Wiktionary, https://ru.wiktionary.org/wiki/червонец.

for close friends and family, and Grandet's circle, where money is the most cherished object. Similarly, diminutives are used in the description of Mr. Prokharchin's treasure in his mattress. Dostoevsky even uses there the same epithet *хорошенькая монета*, "cute little coin." He also employs many other diminutives throughout the description of Mr. Prokharchin's money: *четвертачки*—"little quarter coins," *двугривеннички*—"little twenty-kopeck coins," *пятиалтынничек*—a "little fifty-kopeck piece."

It was already mentioned that Mr. Prokharchin's treasure is a parodic representation of Grandet's gold. While Grandet's coins all have substantial value in francs; Dostoevsky's "little man" treasure consists of coins of a much smaller denomination, and includes lowly copper, along with gold and silver, and even a paper bill. The irony continues in the fact that Eugénie's red purse contains five thousand eight hundred francs, while Mr. Prokharchin's mattress, despite the agitated expectations of other tenants, contains a much lesser sum—only two thousand four hundred and ninety seven rubles.

Even though Mr. Prokharchin has little in common with the Old Grandet except their shared mania of avarice, they both derive a sense of comfort and security in their physical proximity to gold. Mr. Prokharchin refuses to deposit his money in the bank and instead keeps it in his mattress, next to him, even though it is risky because other tenants of the boarding house could rob him. Balzac's Grandet towards the end of his life becomes more and more obsessed with gold as a material substance: "La vue de l'or, la possession de l'or était devenue sa monomanie"[48] (The sight of gold, the possession of gold had become his monomania).[49] This is especially noticeable in the final scenes of the novel, when Grandet is paralyzed and about to die. Even though he no longer can go to his office himself, as he used to do every night, he keeps asking Eugénie to position his wheelchair in front of the doors to his office where he can see the sacs of money that he used to touch and admire.

> Enfin arrivèrent les jours d'agonie, pendant lesquels la forte charpente du bonhomme fut aux prises avec la desctruction. Il voulut rester assis au coin de son feu, devant la porte de son cabinet. Il attirait à lui et roulait toutes les couvertures que l'on mettait sur lui, et disant à Nanon: Serre, serre çà, pour q'on ne me vole pas. Quant il pouvait ouvrir les eyes, où toute sa vie s'était

---

48 Balzac, *Eugénie Grandet*, 320.
49 Idem, *Père Goriot, and Eugénie Grandet*, 459.

réfugiée, il les tournait assitôt vers la porte du cabinet où gisaient ses trésors en disant à sa fille:

> —Y sont-ils! Y sont-ils! d'un son de voix qui dénotait une sorte de peur panique.
>
> —Oui, mon père.
>
> —Veille à l'or, mets de l'or devant moi!

Alors, Eugénie lui étendait des louis sur une petite table, et il demeurait des heures entières, les yeux attachés sur les louis, comme un enfant, qui, au moment où il commence à voir, comtemple stupidment le même objet; et comme à une enfant, il lui échappait un sourire penible.

> —Ça me réchauffe! disait-il quelquefois en laissant paraître sur sa figure une expression de béatitude.[50]

(Finally the death struggle began. The old man's strong frame came to grips with the forces of destruction. He was determined to sit at the chimney corner, facing the door of his office. He drew off and rolled up all the covers that were put over him, saying to Nanon, "Put them away, lock them up, so nobody can steal them." Whenever he could open his eyes, in which all his remaining life had taken refuge, he would turn them toward the door of his office where his treasures lay, and say to his daughter, "Are they there? Are they there?" in a tone of voice which betrayed a kind of panic fear. "Yes, Father."

"Take care of the gold . . . show me some gold!"

Eugénie then would spread louis on a table, and he would remain for hours on end with his eyes fixed on the coins like a child, who, at the moment it begins to see, keeps stupidly staring at the same object. And as with a child, a painful smile would flicker over his face.

"It warms me up!" he would say sometimes, allowing a beatific expression to appear on his countenance.[51]

In Dostoevsky's translation the beginning of this paragraph is omitted and this section begins with the following words:

Старик чувствовал холод, его укрывали одеялами, и он поминутно говорил с судорожным беспокойством "Укройте, укройте меня! Нас обокрадут, обокрадут." Когда же он мог открывать глаза, то устремлял мутный взор на дверь своего кабинета, ощупывал в кармане свой ключ

---

50 Idem, *Eugénie Grandet*, 335–336.
51 Idem, *Père Goriot, and Eugénie Grandet*, 468.

и поминутно шептал своей дочери: "Цело ли золото, цело ли золото?" Потом он приказывал приносить себе золото. Тогда Евгения рассыпала перед ним на столе луидоры. Старик смотрел на них по целым часам, словно дитя, едва начинающее видеть, и, как у дитяти, тягостная улыбка слетала с губ его.

—Это греет меня, мне тепло, мне тепло,—повторял он в каком-то бессмысленном самозабвении.[52]

(The old man felt cold, he was covered with blankets, and he kept saying with a convulsive anxiety: "Cover, cover me! They will rob us, rob us!" When he could open his eyes, he would look at the door of his office with a dull look, feel his key in his pocket and whisper to his daughter every minute: "Is the gold safe, is the gold safe?" Then he would order to bring the gold. Then Evgenia would scatter louis before him on the table. The old man would look at them for hours at a time, as a child who was just beginning to see, and, as from a child, a painful smile flew from his lips.

"It warms me up, I feel warm, I feel warm," he repeated in a meaningless self-oblivion.)[53]

It is easily noticeable that in Dostoevsky's version of this excerpt there are several omissions and substitutions. Not only the important part about the struggle between life and death is omitted entirely, but Dostoevsky's Grandet appears much more frail, and almost senile because he continuous repeats the same words. In Balzac's original, Grandet is still strong (he mentions "the old man's strong frame") and willful ("he was determined to sit at the chimney corner, facing the door of his office"). Grandet demands that the covers be taken off his bed and put away, so that no one can steal them. In Dostoevsky's translation, any references to Grandet's strong frame are absent, and instead Grandet asks for the covers to be put on, because he feels cold. Dostoevsky made this change because he felt that it created a more logical connection with the latter words of Grandet that the sight of gold "warms him up." Moreover, in Russian Grandet's gold is described as *chervontsy* in other parts of the novel, and the word *chervonyi*, as was mentioned above, also connotes the color red, and thus also can be interpreted as a metaphor for fire and warmth.

---

52 Dostoevskii, *Evgeniia Grande*, 197–198.
53 Translation mine.

In Dostoevsky's translation, every minute Grandet checks for his key in his pocket, but in Balzac's original, this sentence is absent because all the keys had already been given to Eugénie several years earlier. Balzac concludes this passage with the description of Grandet's facial expression as Grandet looks at his gold with *une expression de béatitude*. Dostoevsky replaces it with "meaningless self-oblivion,"[54] again highlighting Grandet's weakness and senility at this point and omitting the word *béautitude* since this noun has positive Christian connotation, and for Dostoevsky it is not possible to ascribe any Christian virtues to Grandet's character. Similarly, when Grandet dies, Balzac writes that his last words to Eugénie were to take care of his fortune and that she would give him the account in heaven, "proving by his words that Christianity should be the religion of misers." In the original edition of Dostoevsky's translation in *Repertuar i panteon* in 1844 this sentence is omitted. It may be due to censorship or to Dostoevsky's personal views, since Christianity was the cornerstone of his moral and philosophical beliefs.

Grandet's cynical view of life as a business is explicitly formulated in the scene where he asks Eugénie to renounce her share of her mother's inheritance after her mother's passing. This is the moment in the novel when even his old friend, the notary Cruchot, appears shocked by Grandet's indifference to the death of his wife and his callousness towards his daughter, as he pressures her to sign the deed renouncing her inheritance. Contrary to her father's obsession with money, Eugénie is completely indifferent to it and she obediently gives her signature. Grandet is overjoyed and he thanks her: "There, my child, you've restored your father's life; but you're only giving him what he gave you. We are quits. That's the way to do business. Life is a business."[55]

Dostoevsky condemns Grandet's cruelty and cupidity and amplifies Grandet's emotions in his translation. He translates this passage in the following manner: "Дитя мое, кровь моя, ты спасла жизнь отцу своему; ты отдашь ему то, что он дал тебе; мы сквитались, ты ничего не должна мне более; вот как делаются дела, Крюшо! Ведь вся жизнь человеческая—сделка и спекуляция, друг мой"[56] (My child, my blood, you have saved your father's life; you will give him what he gave you; we are

---

54 Balzac, *Père Goriot, and Eugénie Grandet*, 467.
55 Balzac, *Père Goriot, and Eugénie Grandet*, 465.
56 Dostoevskii, *Evgeniia Grande*, 194–195.

even, you owe me nothing more; that's how things are done, Cruchot! After all, the whole human life is a transaction and speculation, my friend).

We immediately note the repetition in Grandet's speech in Russian, as he addresses Evgenia not only as his daughter, but as his blood, emphatically stressing their family bond. Then, by choosing to say that she *saved* his life, rather than restored, Dostoevsky once again conveys to the reader that money is always a matter of life or death for Grandet. There are two more emphatic repetitions in the Russian translation, when Grandet says that they are even, and Evgenia owes him nothing more (Dostoevsky's added phrase). The mentioning of "owing nothing" here has a double meaning: on the one hand, one can talk about children owing love and care to their parents in exchange for the care they received as babies; on the other hand, in Grandet's world of bills and business deals, the verb "to owe" has a very direct meaning tied to specific monetary amounts. Dostoevsky emphasizes Grandet's view of the whole life as a business venture. Instead of saying that life is a business, as Grandet does in the original, in Russian, Grandet says that life is a transaction and a speculation (*сделка и спекуляция*). Choosing these two words, Dostoevsky passes a strongly critical judgment on his character, since both words in Russian have a negative connotation: *сделка* means "a bargain, a deal," and it is used in fixed expressions such as "a pact with the Devil" (*сделка с Дьяволом*), "a compromise with one's conscience" (*сделка с совестью*), and so forth. *Спекуляция* is even worse, because it usually describes raising a price beyond the true value of an item or unscrupulous profiteering over someone who does not suspect it.

The Value of Money in Evgenia Grande and The Gambler (1867)

The multi-tiered value system of gold coins that first appears in the description of Eugénie's purse, and the difference between the actual value and the symbolic value of money is something that Dostoevsky later actively employed in his own novels. In *The Gambler* (1867), money functions at the symbolic level as the indicator of characters' personal worth, pride, and freedom. One of the central scenes of the novel is set at the casino in the fictional town of Rulettenburg where the protagonist Alexei Ivanovich needs to win fifty thousand francs for the woman he loves, Polina, to set her free from her former lover de Grieux who lent her the money earlier. De Grieux is now threatening Polina with the promissory notes received from the general, her stepfather. Upon Polina's request, Alexei goes to the casino and unexpectedly wins two hundred thousand francs in an hour, but this money is only important in the context of his relationship with Polina. He returns triumphantly to his hotel room, where Polina has been waiting for him, and offers her the money, but she refuses to take it at first, saying that the mistress of de Grieux is not worth fifty thousand francs. After they spend the night together, Polina takes his fifty thousand francs only to throw it into Alexei's face.

Money here functions as a symbol of human dignity and pride, and for that reason it is so important for Polina to be able to repay de Grieux. At the same time, she is uncomfortable taking money from Alexei to accomplish her goal, so she becomes his mistress to replicate outwardly the situation with de Grieux, although she knows that Alexei genuinely loves her. After that climactic scene in the hotel, Polina runs away in great distress to Mr. Astley whose role in the novel is that of a benevolent protector and benefactor. Another effect of Alexei's miraculous win in the casino is on the demimondaine mademoiselle Blanche, who has been living with Polina's stepfather and was going to marry him. She abruptly changes her mind about the general and goes instead with Alexei to Paris to squander his new fortune.

After his first phantasmagorical experience at the gaming tables, Alexei becomes addicted to gambling, and after his money is gone in two months he returns to the casino, but this time luck is no longer on his side. After more than a year of unsuccessfully trying to rebuild his fortune and even spending some time in debtors' prison, he writes in his diary:

О, не деньги мне дороги! Я уверен, что разбросал бы их опять какой-нибудь Blanche и опять ездил бы в Париже три недели на паре собственных лошадей в шестнадцать тысяч франков. Я ведь наверное знаю, что не скуп, а между тем, однако ж, с каким трепетом я выслушиваю крик крупера . . . с какой алчностью смотрю я на игорный стол, по которому разбросаны луидоры, фридрихсдоры и талеры, на столбики золота, когда они от лопатки крупера рассыпаются в горящие, как жар, кучи, или на длинные в аршин столбы серебра, лежащие вокруг колеса.[57]

(No, I had no desire for money for its own sake, for I was perfectly well aware that I should only squander it upon some new Blanche, and spend

---

57 Dostoevskii, *Sobranie sochinenii v 12 tomakh*, 3:438.

another three weeks in Paris after buying a pair of horses which had cost sixteen thousand francs. No, I never believed myself to be a hoarder; in fact, I knew only too well that I was a spendthrift. And already, with a sort of fear, a sort of sinking in my heart, I could hear the cries of the croupiers. . . . How greedily I gazed upon the gaming-table, with its scattered louis d'or, ten-gulden pieces, and thalers; upon the streams of gold as they issued from the croupier's hands, and piled themselves up into heaps of gold scintillating as fire; upon the long rolls of silver lying around the croupier.)[58]

In this passage at the end of the novel, we see the intense voyeuristic pleasure of looking at the gold and silver coins similar to the one experienced by Balzac's Grandet. The central character of *The Gambler* after his magical win joined the *francmaçonnerie des passions* and also became a monomaniac obsessed with a single passion: gambling. He repeats that the purchasing power of the money is not what is important to him ("не деньги мне дороги")[59], and says that he would squander it again easily, but his heart leaps when he sees the piles of gold and silver coins on the table. Like Grandet, he is overtaken by the beauty and radiance of coins that physically represent wealth. In this passage, the reader also sees the main character meticulously enumerate the coins of various denominations that are spread on the gaming table, just like Eugénie's gold coins have been counted earlier, with slight changes—Alexei mentions German thalers and Prussian gold coins in addition to French louis d'or. Thus, *The Gambler* is connected to *Eugénie Grandet* by its treatment of money as, at the same time, a material object and a symbol of the monomania of the central character.

The Gambler is also connected with *Le Père Goriot*, one of Dostoevsky's favorite novels by Balzac on the plot level. In Balzac's novel, Delphine de Nucingen sends Eugène de Rastignac to gamble at the Palais Royal to win her six thousand francs, which she needs to pay back to her lover de Marsay. Dostoevsky replicated this plot episode in a similar scene between Polina and Alexei Ivanovich in *The Gambler*. Polina has compromised herself by coming to Alexei's hotel room to ask for his help to obtain the fifty thousand francs. Similarly, Delphine has also risked her reputation by going in her carriage with Rastignac to the Palais Royale and trusting him with her secret of owing six thousand francs to de Marsay, and Rastignac is aware of

58 Fyodor Dostoyevsky, *The Gambler*, trans. C. J. Hogarth, https://www.gutenberg.org/files/2197/2197-h/2197-h.htm.

59 Dostoevskii, *Sobranie sochinenii v 12 tomakh*, 3:438.

his power over her. Exactly like Alexei Ivanovich in *The Gambler*, Rastignac has never gambled before, so when he comes to the gambling table, he feels dazzled and does not understand the rules of the game, but he is in love, so he only thinks of the woman he loves and hopes to conquer her heart by winning the money she needs. Luck is on his side, and he unexpectedly wins seven thousand francs at roulette by betting first on twenty-one, his age (Alexei bets on twenty-two) and then on red, just like Dostoevsky's character. In parallel to the situation in *The Gambler*, after his win at the casino, Rastignac also gets Delphine's love, and his position in society radically changes, as do his personal beliefs. Thus, money in both of these works becomes a litmus test for the characters' inner strength and integrity. Moreover, in both novels money is also the characters' primary motivator for action. In *The Gambler*, these actions lead to disastrous results—a gambling addiction for Alexei. In Balzac's novel, on the contrary, Rastignac achieves personal success manifested by his rapid rise through the ranks of Parisian society.

In *The Gambler* and in *Le Père Goriot* money becomes a placeholder for emotions, the embodiment of love, pride, or passion. In *Eugénie Grandet*, Old Grandet's entire life revolves around accumulating his fortune, which also replaces his family relationships and any other human connections. At the same time, his daughter and wife are not concerned with money at all, even though it was his wife's dowry and then inheritance from the relatives on her side that became the cornerstone of Grandet's wealth. Madame Grandet and Eugénie believe that he does not have any money.

> Eugénie et sa mère ne savaient rien de la fortune de Grandet. Elles n'estimaient les choses de la vie qu'à la lueur de leurs pâles idées, et ne prisaient ni ne méprisaient l'argent; ells etaient accoutumées à s'en passer. Leurs sentiments, frossées a leur insu, mais vivaces, le secret de leur existence, en faisaient des exceptions curieuses dans cette réunion de gens dont la vie était purement matérielle.[60]

> (Eugénie and her mother knew nothing of Grandet's fortune; they judged the world only in the light of their own vague notions, and neither valued nor despised money, because they were used to doing without it. Their feelings, repressed without their knowledge, yet still surviving, and the isolation of

---

60 Balzac, *Eugénie Grandet*, 77.

their existence, made them curious exceptions in this gathering of people for whom only the material things counted.)[61]

For Eugénie, unlike her father, money has no importance. It only exists for her in the context of her feelings, and she is momentarily content to have it as she counts her gold because it enables her to help Charles. As Alexei and Rastignac, Eugénie also uses money to support the person she loves, but when Charles goes away, it loses any value for her. After the death of her father, she inherits twenty million francs and becomes a very rich woman. But this great change in her fortune leaves her completely indifferent, and she continues to maintain the extremely simple and frugal lifestyle of her father.

> Eugénie commençait à souffrir. Pour elle, la fortune n'était ni un pouvoir, ni une consolation. Elle ne pouvait exister que par l'amour, par la religion, par sa foi dans l'avenir. L'amour lui expliquait l'éternité. Son coeur et L'Evangile lui signalaient deux mondes à attendre. Elle se plongeait nuit et jour au sein de deux pensées infinies, qui, pour elle, peut-être n'en faisaient qu'une seule. Elle se retirait en elle-même, aimant et se croyant aimée. Depuis sept ans, sa passion avait tout envahit. Ses trésors n'étaient pas les vingt millions dont elle entassait insouciamment les revenues, mais le coffret de Charles, mais les deux portraits suspendues à son lit, mais les bijoux rachetés à son père, étalés orgueilleusement sur une couche de ouate dans un tiroir du bahut; mais le dé de sa tante dont s'était servi sa mère, et que tous les jours elle prenait religieusement pour travailler à une broderie, ouvrage de Pénélope, entrepris seulement pour mettre à son doigt cet or plein de souvenirs.[62]

> (Eugénie had begun to suffer. In her case wealth was neither a power nor a consolation; she could only exist through love, through religion and through her faith in the future. Love made her understand eternity. Her heart and the gospel marked out two worlds awaiting her. Night and day she was plunged in the depth of human thoughts, which for her perhaps merged into one. She withdrew into herself, loving and believing herself loved. For seven years her passion had filled everything for her. Her treasures were not the millions from which the income was piling up, but Charles's dressing-case, the two portraits hanging above her bed, the jewels recovered from her father and proudly spread out on a layer of cotton wool in a drawer of the chest, her

---

61 Balzac, *Père Goriot, and Eugénie Grandet*, 323.
62 Balzac, *Eugénie Grandet*, 342.

aunt's thimble, which her mother had used and which she put on religiously every day to work at a piece of embroidery—Penelope's web, begun solely for the purpose of wearing on her finger that gold so full of memories.

In Dostoevsky's translation, greater emphasis is placed on Evgenia's long suffering linking her to Christian martyrs, rather than on Penelope's hopeful waiting for the return of Odysseus. Dostoevsky omitted the reference to Penelope and instead emphasized Evgenia's faith and religion, and the potential of rewards in the future as a consolation for suffering endured on earth.

Евгения страдала; для нее мало значили ее сокровище, ее несметное богатство. Она жила в будущем идеей, верой, любовью—своей религией. Любовь, как уверяло сердце ее, существовала и в вечности. Сердце ее и Евангелие раскрывали ей в будущем два мира. Денно и нощно погружалась она в стихию двух безбрежных идей, составлявших для нее, быть может, единую мысль. Она углублялась в самое себя, любя и веря, что она любима. И семь лет, семь лет любви, заняли всю ее жизнь, все надежды, все стремления. Не миллионы, оставленные отцом ее, были ее сокровищами, но ларец Шарля, но два портрета, висевшие над ее постелью, но драгоценности его, выкупленные у отца и теперь горделиво блиставшие на ватной подстилке в одном из ящиков ее комода, наконец, наперсток матери, подаренный Шарлем. И каждый день садилась Евгения за работу, за нескончаемую работу свою, только для того, чтобы почувствовать на своем пальце этот кусочек золота, навевающий столько воспоминаний.[63]

In Dostoevsky's translation there are several substantial changes. Instead of using "wealth," he uses the word *сокровище* (treasure) twice, creating a textual parallel between Evgenia's financial wealth that he also calls "treasure," and her true treasure consisting of the items that are connected to Charles—the portraits of his parents, his jewelry, and the thimble that he gave to her mother. This textual juxtaposition of the two "treasures"—her material wealth and sentimental objects left by Charles highlights the fact that Evgenia only cherishes his gifts because they remind her of him and his time spent with her, and that is what she considers her true treasure. The specifics of her fortune (twenty millions plus ever-increasing revenues) are not mentioned at all, instead Dostoevsky vaguely says that she had *несметные*

---

63 Dostoevskii, *Evgeniia Grande*, 201–202.

богатства—countless riches, using a cliché frequently used in fairytales, and also several times in the Bible. Countless riches, or infinite riches, are promised to the faithful in the Kingdom of God after they leave the earthly realm (Luke 6:35), but Dostoevsky gives "innumerable riches" to Evgenia during her life, not after death. In this way, he strengthens her spiritual connection to Heaven and emphasizes the saintly qualities that she has already attained by her numerous virtuous deeds and deep religious faith.

Just as Dostoevsky's Grandet is treated as the archetype of an old miser, Dostoevsky's Evgenia is portrayed as a saint, and her involvement in earthly matters (for example, collecting revenues from her millions) is attenuated, while her connection to God is emphasized. In Balzac's original, Eugénie lives through her love, her religion, and her faith in the future. Dostoevsky combines these three spiritual spheres into one, saying instead that Evgenia lived in the future through her faith and love, which she equated to religion. Balzac's words that through love Eugénie understood eternity, Dostoevsky changes to "love for her existed in eternity," again emphasizing the future celestial life and its potential rewards, not here but also in eternity. In Balzac's original, love occupies the whole world of Eugénie and becomes her religion, and he even uses the adverb *religieusement*—"religiously," when he talks about her daily use of the thimble that Charles gave to her mother. Dostoevsky omits this adverb here since he does not see the reason for using it out of its proper context. Dostoevsky also omits the reference to Penelope that in Balzac's text evokes not only her daily weaving, deliberately never finished, but also many years of faithful waiting. Instead, he uses repetition to emphasize Evgenia's unwavering daily practice: "и каждый день садилась Евгения за работу, за нескончаемую работу свою" (and every day Evgenia sat down to her work, to her endless work). Repetition here and in the earlier instance (*и семь лет, семь лет любви*—"and seven years, seven years of love") gives the narrative at this moment in the text a special style imitating the oral tradition (*skaz* in Russian). In *skaz* the narrator deliberately abandons literary style and imitates oral speech, as if talking a listener while the story unfolds in its telling.[64] This style also implies an actively involved audience and it draws the reader into the narrative. The use of the oral register (*skaz*) creates a particular literary effect of juxtaposing

---

64 For more see Viktor Vinogradov, *O iazyke khudozhestvennoi prozy* (Moscow, Russia: Nauka, 1980).

the literary style of the author and the conversational stylized register of the narrator side by side in the text. By introducing this other stylized narrative voice in the text, young Dostoevsky creates a two-voiced narrative predating his own polyphonic novels. Other examples of *skaz* in the Russian literature can be found in Nikolai Leskov's works, Pavel Bazhov's tales, and Mikhail Zoshchenko's short stories.

The Symbolic Value of Money in Eugénie Grandet and The Idiot (1868)

As was already mentioned, in *Eugénie Grandet* money functions on multiple levels. On the real level, it is a commodity for Grandet and his neighbors Cruchots and Grassins, and on the symbolic level, it is the focus of Grandet's mania and a tool of love for his daughter and mother. Dostoevsky also applied this multi-tiered approach to money in many of his great novels. One of the characters for whom money has only symbolic value, divorced of its outward appearance, is Nastasya Filippovna in *The Idiot*. Nastasya Filippovna is a stunningly beautiful courtesan who was raped when she was a sixteen-year-old orphan by a rich nobleman, Totsky, and continued to live with him and to take money from him for a number of years before the beginning of the novel. From the conventional viewpoint shared by her salon visitors, because of her social standing as a kept woman, Nastasya Filippovna is perceived as someone to whom money has a great value, and like everyone else's, her behavior and actions should be greatly influenced by it.

These notions are completely overturned in one of the culminating scenes of the novel at Nastasya Filippovna's nameday party in her apartment in Saint Petersburg. Nastasya Filippovna is expected to make an announcement about her upcoming marriage to Ganya, to whom Totsky promised seventy-five thousand rubles for marrying Nastasya and thus freeing Totsky of any obligations towards her. However, Nastasya Filippovna rejects Ganya. She throws a hundred thousand rubles that Rogozhin has offered her to become his mistress into the fireplace and offers Ganya to keep the money if he is able to salvage the banknotes from the fire:

Ну, так слушай же, Ганя, я хочу на твою душу в последний раз посмотреть; ты меня сам целые три месяца мучил; теперь мой черед. Видишь ты эту пачку, в ней сто тысяч! Вот я ее сейчас брошу в камин, в огонь, вот при всех, все свидетели! Как только огонь обхватит ее всю, —

полезай в камин, но только без перчаток, с голыми руками, и рукава отверни, и тащи пачку из огня! Вытащишь—твоя, все сто тысяч твои![65]

(Well then, listen, Ganya, I want to look at your soul for the last time; you've tormented me for a whole three months; now it's my turn. Do you see this parcel, it contains a hundred thousand! In a moment I am going to throw it into the fireplace, into the flames, in front of everyone, there're all witnesses! As soon as the flames catch hold of it—crawl into the fireplace, but without gloves, mind, with your bare hands, your sleeves rolled up, and pull the parcel out of the fire! If you pull it out it's yours, the whole hundred thousand is yours!)[66]

In this emotionally turbulent scene, Dostoevsky uses money as a test for the main characters, similar to the creative technique that Balzac employed in *Eugénie Grandet* when describing the conflict between Grandet and Eugénie over her gold, discussed earlier. The attitude toward money depicted in this crucial scene reveals Nastasya Filippovna's complete indifference to it and the baseness and pettiness of Ganya, who, according to Rogozhin's words, would "crawl to Vasilievsky Island for three silver rubles." In this instance, Ganya manages to restrain himself from reaching into the fireplace but ends up fainting from emotional tension.

While Nastasya Filippovna's coterie views her behavior as mad, Rogozhin, whose money she threw into the fire, is very impressed with her high-mindedness and royal disregard for money. He calls Nastasya Filippovna his queen and dares anybody in the room to repeat her action. During this eventful evening, Prince Myshkin also makes the unexpected announcement that he has inherited one and a half million rubles from an aunt, and proposes to Nastasya Filippovna. She rejects his proposal and goes into the night with Rogozhin, leaving the stack of the hundred thousand rubles that she rescued from the fire next to Ganya as a "reward" for his ability to restrain himself from reaching into the flames.

Thus, in the course of a single evening, Nastasya Filippovna returned to Totsky the seventy-five thousand rubles that he was going to pay for her upcoming marriage with Ganya, gave away Rogozhin's hundred thousand rubles to Ganya, and refused Prince Myshkin's proposal together with his fortune of one and a half million rubles.

---

65 Dostoevskii, *Sobranie sochinenii v 15 tomakh*, 6:185.

66 Dostoyevsky, *The Idiot*, 201.

The quantities of money, which Nastasya Filippovna had been offered and rejected over the course of a single evening, represent a staggering amount for the nineteenth-century reader. To better understand the amount of money that Nastasya Filippovna threw into the fire, one can look at the documented account of Dostoevsky's financial situation that he described in one of his letters in 1867 while traveling in Europe with his wife. In his letter, he thanks his friend and doctor S. Yanovsky for sending him one hundred rubles that in Dostoevsky's own words "pulled him out of trouble, although only for some time"[67] ("вытащили меня из беды, правда только на некоторое время").[68] He continues the letter saying that he still owes four thousand rubles to the literary journal *Russkii vestnik* that paid his honorarium in advance. He already spent this money as he organized his wedding, covered other small debts, made some other expenses, and paid for his trip abroad with his wife. One can see from that description that four thousand rubles represented quite a lot of money, and a hundred thousand rubles was a very impressive sum indeed. The staggering amount of money lost and gained also connects *The Idiot* with *Eugénie Grandet* where, according to Balzac's sister Laure Surville, there were "too many millions,"[69] and Balzac in subsequent editions worked to reduce the size of Grandet's fortune to make it more realistic.

Prince Myshkin's reaction to his newly inherited wealth is similar to Nastasya Filippovna's demonstrated indifference to monetary rewards. He only mentions his changed financial situation in light of his possible marriage to Nastasya Filippovna, and he does it in a very casual manner. When he begins his proposal, he first talks about his love, deep admiration, and respect for Nastasya Filippovna. Only when others begin to laugh at his words, he shows the letter that reveals his inheritance.

These two characters are portrayed in a stark contrast to the rest of the society at the party. One of the guests, Ferdyshchenko, offers to fetch the money from the flames with his teeth for one thousand rubles, and General Yepanchin at the end of the night, even after all the tumultuous events, remembers to take back a very expensive pearl necklace, which he has brought to Nastasya Filippovna as a nameday present.

Rogozhin also stands apart from the rest of the guests, but for a different reason. Unlike other guests, he views money not as a goal in itself, but as

---

67 Translation mine.
68 Fedor Dostoevskii, *Pis'ma (1866)*, http://www.litmir.me/br/?b=121132&p=29.
69 See Surville and Balzac, *Balzac, sa vie et ses oeuvres d'apres sa correspondance*, 157.

an effective tool, as a merchant would, to buy what he wants: a night of love with Nastasya Filippovna. For him, however, money is always subordinate to passion, and for that reason he admires Nastasya Filippovna's actions that night. While everybody else thinks that she has gone mad, Rogozhin sees in her an open disdain for society's expectations and norms of behavior, similar to his own.

> Сам Рогожин весь обратился в один неподвижный взгляд. Он оторваться не мог от Настасьи Филипповны, он упивался, он был на седьмом небе.
>
> —Вот это так королева!—повторял он поминутно, обращаясь кругом к кому ни попало,—вот это так по-нашему!—вскрикивал он, не помня себя.—Ну, кто из вас, мазурики, такую штуку сделает, а?[70]

(Rogozhin himself had turned into a single, motionless stare. He was unable to tear himself away from Nastasya Filippovna, he was intoxicated, he was in seventh heaven. "That's how a queen behaves!" he repeated every moment, addressing whomever happened to be around. "That's how our kind behaves!" he shrieked, beside himself. "Well, which of you swindlers would do a thing like that, eh?")[71]

Rogozhin's words illustrate his belief in living large. He admires Nastasya Filippovna for her ability to follow her passions, and her disregard for conventional norms of behavior. In his speech he unites her and himself ("that's the way our kind behaves"), sensing in her the same passionate nature and conjuring up the popular legendary accounts of daredevilry and recklessness of the Russian merchants. But ultimately, the extreme passions of Rogozhin and his inability to restrain his jealousy are the cause of the tragic finale of the novel—Rogozhin murders Nastasya Filippovna, which triggers the return of Prince Myshkin's illness. *The Idiot* closely intertwines the themes of money, morality, generosity, and love, continuing Balzac's novelistic tradition transplanted into the context of the nineteenth-century Russian society and Dostoevsky's personal beliefs and values.

This chapter has focused on the comparative study of the money theme in *Eugénie Grandet* and its treatment in Dostoevsky's free translation. It has also studied the subsequent development and permutations of the money

---

70 Dostoevskii, *Sobranie sochinenii v 12 tomakh*, 6:187.
71 Dostoevsky, *The Idiot*, 203.

theme in Dostoevsky's own works and their shared elements with Balzac's novels. It has demonstrated that in the works of both authors, Dostoevsky and Balzac, money functions on multiple levels: it is not only a physical indicator of wealth, but also a litmus test for a character's integrity, and the complexity of money matters is directly connected to the inner workings of family relationships and love. For both authors, money plays a central role in plot development, and the attitude of their characters to money is directly related to their moral values and actions.

At the same time, there are some stark differences in the treatment of money between the two authors. In Balzac's fictional world, money as the object of desire generally fuels the characters' ambitions and motivates their actions. In Zweig's assessment, it permeates "vicissitudes of other passions . . . manipulating all the urges of human nature."[72] While Dostoevsky agreed with Balzac in viewing money as a very influential agent in human behavior, in Dostoevsky's system of ethical values love of money becomes the sign of corruptibility, immorality, and even psychological deviation, as in the case of Mr. Prokharchin.

For both Balzac and Dostoevsky, a woman's ability to love manifests itself in readiness to sacrifice her material wealth. The character's ability to rise above the material world and renounce its financial advantages for love is something that young Dostoevsky admired in Balzac's Eugénie, and he created his most compelling female characters following this model.

---

72 Zweig, *Balzac, Dickens, Dostoevsky: Master Builders of the Spirit*, 45.

Conclusion

This book has presented a close reading of Dostoevsky's translation against its French original, which has uncovered many discrepancies, additions, and substitutions in the Russian text. It has also shown how these changes have affected the Russian readers' understanding of Balzac's novel.

In addition, this comparative study has brought into focus the profound resemblance between the two authors that lies at the core of their poetics, visible already in young Dostoevsky's work as a translator of Balzac's text. The echoes and interactions between them can be traced on many levels: in shared plots, ideas, narrative strategies, and on the broader scale, in ethical and philosophical dilemmas posed in their works. The complex interconnection between Balzac and Dostoevsky affects our understanding of nineteenth-century European culture and creates a broader picture of nineteenth-century humanist values. This analysis has highlighted many features of literary style and poetics that young Dostoevsky appropriated from Balzac's *Eugénie Grandet* and transplanted onto Russian soil in his own writing: the *théorie du milieu*; the psychological analysis of avarice as a monomaniac passion; the archetypes of selfless, deeply loving women and extreme misers, whose passion for avarice borders on disease; the motifs of complete self-sacrifice and betrayal; and the ultimate reversal of fortune. Studying Dostoevsky's free translation of Balzac as his first published literary work, we have identified certain precursors of his own literary style, such as Dostoevsky's focus on the psychological development of the characters; the underlying tension of an ongoing silent family drama; the dialogic nature of the narrator directly addressing the readers; and the intense contradictions between heart and reason—a life guided by all-encompassing love, like that of Eugénie, and a life subordinated to calculations and money, like that of her father.

The character of Eugénie, shaped by complete self-sacrifice, religious faith, compassion, and depth of feelings, made a profound impact

Dostoevsky who followed this model to create his own idealized female characters, such as Alexandra Mikhailovna in *Netochka Nezvanova* (1848), Sonya in *Crime and Punishment* (1866), Sophia in *The Raw Youth* (1875), the unnamed female character in "The Meek One" (1876), and Alyosha's mother in *The Brothers Karamazov* (1880). All these characters embodied the Christian concept of meek resistance, first mentioned by Dostoevsky in his translation of Balzac's novel in regards to Evgenia (*krotkoe sopro-tivlenie*) and not found in Balzac's original. For Dostoevsky, it was a very valuable spiritual trait, as it allowed a person to maintain integrity and high moral standards in the face of adverse circumstances. Consequently, he bestowed this prized quality upon his most-beloved female characters. The motif of meekness and non-resistance, viewed as inner strength and nurtured by religious faith, is also found in other Russian novels, for example, in Tolstoy's portrayal of Princess Maria in *War and Peace*. The defining feature of Christian meekness as a strength can further be seen in several other major female characters from the Russian literary tradition, not only in Tolstoy, but also in Chekhov's works, such as Sonya in *Uncle Vanya* and Lipa in "In the Ravine" (1899).

A study of avarice as a monomania and its destructive effects on human personality, embodied in the character of Old Grandet, was another element of Balzac's novel that Dostoevsky found very intriguing from the psychological viewpoint. He later explored the monomaniacal passions and their consequences in many of his stories and novels, such as "Mr. Prokharchin," written in 1846, shortly after he finished the translation. In this story, the theme of extreme avarice is treated as a parody. Its main character is Mr. Prokharchin, or "Mr. Aboutsoup," a little clerk leading anabnormally frugal life in one of the squalid boarding houses in Saint Petersburg. Mr. Prokharchin is a caricature of Balzac's "superior"[1] character, the Old Grandet who always surpassed his neighbors in intelligence and business acumen. Like Grandet, though, Mr. Prokharchin derives a sense of security from his physical proximity to his money.

Dostoevsky, like Balzac, viewed money as an extremely influential factor in human behavior. He investigated the closely connected relationship of money and human conduct in several of his major works, such as *Crime and Punishment*, *The Gambler*, *The Brothers Karamazov*, and "The

---

1   See Hyppolite Taine, *Balzac, a Critical Study*, trans. Lorenzo o'Rourke (Folcroft, PA: Folcroft Library Editions, 1973), 206.

Meek One." The understanding of money as the inner spring behind all human actions and decisions is openly declared in *Eugénie Grandet*, when Grandet says to Cruchot that "all human life is a transaction." Dostoevsky amplified this statement by adding an extra word to Grandet's pronouncement: "and a speculation" (*и спекуляция*), thus drawing the readers' attention to the centrality of this motif in Balzac's novel, and setting it up as a future leitmotif in his own writing. In the world of *La Comédie humaine*, a strong desire to build a fortune to be able to afford a life of elegance and luxury typically impels to action characters such as Eugène de Rastignac and Lucien de Rubempré. In Dostoevsky's novelistic world, on the contrary, the love of money is always sinful and leads characters into moral degradation or addiction, like the pawnbroker in "The Meek One" or Alexei in *The Gambler*. The ability to resist temptation in the form of proffered wealth becomes a litmus test for the character's integrity and spiritual worth, such as for Nastasya Filippovna's in *The Idiot* or the unnamed female character of "The Meek One."

Both, Balzac and Dostoevsky, can be viewed as chroniclers not only of nineteenth-century life but of the human psyche. Alex de Jonge noted that Dostoevsky "does not seek realistic representation, he depicts the psyche of the world. He writes not the history of the nineteenth century but its mythology."[2] Just as Dostoevsky created the myth of Petersburg,[3] Balzac is also viewed as a creator of the myth of Paris and a chronicler of the contemporary nineteenth-century man looking for answers to the ethical and moral dilemmas posed by the emerging new realities of the day. New social and economic trends, related to the shift from feudal to capitalist mode of production, and their subsequent effects on moral norms and codes of behavior found their reflections in many of the novels of *La Comédie humaine*. *Eugénie Grandet* is one of several novels juxtaposing the old bourgeois lifestyle, embodied by Grandet, and his traditional ways of making money through land and vineyards, with the new, faster pace of life in the metropolis and the illusory quick wealth existing on paper only, embodied by Charles and his father. The gradual erosion and disappearance of old beliefs, and the anxiety of the contemporary man searching for meaning of life in the new social order, are also central to Dostoevsky's world view. His characters grapple with the same philosophical dilemmas, as is

---

2   Alex de Jonge, *Dostoevsky and the Age of Intensity* (New York: St. Martin Press, 1975), 2.
3   For more, see Fanger, *Dostoevsky and Romantic Realism*.

the case with Raskolnikov in *Crime and Punishment*, Ivan in *The Brothers Karamazov*, Arkady and Versilov in *The Raw Youth*.

We have seen that young Dostoevsky left an indelible mark on Balzac's original text of *Eugénie Grandet* and adapted it in a way that he felt was best for Russian readers. He "transplanted" the French original into the Russian culture by bringing the text to the reader and facilitating understanding of the French novel by average Russian readers, rather than providing an exact translation. At the same time, as he was "inscribing himself"[4] into Balzac's text, consciously or perhaps even unconsciously,[5] he appropriated many of the features of Balzac's style that he later used in his own writing. Thus, his translation also merits our special attention because in Dostoevsky's first published text we can see how his work as translator becomes a starting point for his new writings later on. A successful translation, such as Dostoevsky's *Evgenia Grandet*, should be considered as a part of a literary legacy of a particular author, along with his own writings, as was demonstrated in our analysis of Dostoevsky's free translation of Balzac.

---

4   See Lawrence Venuti, *The Translator's Invisibility. A History of Translation* (London and New York. Routledge, 1995), 21.

5   For more on unsconscious memory manifesting itself later, see Daniel Schacter, *Searching for Memory: The Brain, the Mind, and the Past* (New York: Basic Books, 1996).

Bibliography

Abraham, Pierre. *Créatures chez Balzac*. Paris, France: Gallimard, Éditions De La Nouvelle Revue Française, 1931.

Apter, Emily. *The Translation Zone*. Princeton, NJ: Princeton University Press, 2006.

Azov, Andrei. *Poverzhennye bykvalisty*. Moscow, Russia: Izdatel'skii dom Vysshei Shkoly Ekonomiki, 2013.

Baer, Brian James, and Susanna Witt, ed. *Translation in Russian Contexts*. New York, NY: Routledge, 2018.

Baer, Brian James. *Translation and the Making of Modern Russian Literature*. New York, NY: Bloomsbury Academic, 2015.

Balzac, Honore de. *César Birotteau*. Paris: Gallimard, 1975.

———. *La Comédie humaine: Études de moeurs: Scènes de la vie privée*. Vol. 2. Edited by Marcel Bouteron. Paris: Gallimard, 1948.

———. *Eugénie Grandet*. Paris: Mme. Charles-Béchet, 1834.

———. *Gobseck et une double famille*. Paris: Éditions Flammarion, 2002.

———. *Illusions perdues*. Paris: Livre de Poche, 2006.

———. *La Fille aux yeux d'or*. Lausanne: Éditions Rencontre, 1968.

———. *Lettres à l'étrangère*. Edited by Saint-John Perse and Mauricette Berne. Paris: Gallimard, 1987.

———. *La Maison Nucingen*. Paris: Gallimard Education, 1989.

———. *Père Goriot, and Eugénie Grandet*. New York: Modern Library, 1950.

———. *Traité de la vie élégante suivi du code de la toilette*. Paris: Édition De L'Amateur, 2012.

———. "L'Avant-propos de 'La Comédie humaine.'" In his *Oeuvres completes*. Paris: Les Bibliophiles de l'originale, 1965.

———. *Une Tenebreuse affaire*. Gallimard, 1973.

Bardèche, Maurice. *Balzac, Romancier*. Paris: Plon, 1947.

Beaujour, Elizabeth. *Alien Tongues*. Ithaka, NY: Cornell University Press, 1989.

Benz, Ernst, Richard Winston, and Clara Winston. *The Eastern Orthodox Church, Its Thought and Life*. Garden City, NY: Anchor Books, 1963.

Bibleiskaiia Enciclopediia Brokgauza. Edited by Fritz Rineker and Gerhardt Meyer. Moscow: Rossiiskoe Bibleiskoe Obschestvo, 1999.

Bloom, Harold, ed. *Honoré de Balzac*. Broomwall, PA: Chelsea House Publishers, 2003.

Brooks, Peter. *Realist Vision*. New Haven, CT: Yale University Press, 2008.

Borges, Jorge Louis. "The Thousand and One Nights." Translated by Eliot Weinberger. *The Georgian Review* (Fall 1984): 564–574.

Castex, Pierre-Georges. "L'ascension de Monsieur Grandet." In his *Horizons Romantiques*, 111–125. Paris, France: Corti, 1983.

———. "Evolution du texte." In *Eugenie Grandet*. Edited and commentaries by Pierre-Georges Castex, 274–287. Paris: Garnier, 1965.

Dictionnaires Larousse français monolingue et bilingues en ligne. Larousse, January 1, 2011. https://www.larousse.fr/dictionnaires/francais.

Dostoevskaia (Snitkina), Anna Grigor'evna. *Vospominaniia, 1846–1917: Solntse moei zhizni, Fedor Dostoevskii*. Moscow, Russia: Boslen, 2015.

Dostoevskii i tret' e tysiacheletie. Sbornik Statei, Moscow: MGOGI, 2012.

Dostoevskii, Fedor, trans. *Evgenia Grandet* by Honore de Balzac. Saint Petersburg, Russia: Azbuka, 2014. Original publication 1844.

Dostoevskii, Fedor. "Gospodin Prokharchin." In his *Polnoe sobranie sochinenii i pisem*, vol. 1, 275–301. Saint Petersburg, Russia: Nauka, 2013.

———[Fyodor Dostoevsky]. *Crime and Punishment: A Novel in Six Parts with Epilogue*. Translated by Richard Pevear and Larissa Volokhonsky. New York: Vintage, 1993.

———[Fyodor Dostoevsky]. *The Brothers Karamazov: A Novel in Four Parts with Epilogue*. Translated by Richard Pevear and Larissa Volokhonsky. New York: Random House, 1991.

———[Fyodor Dostoevsky]. *The Idiot*. Translated by David McDuff. London: Penguin, 2004.

———[Fyodor Dostoevsky]. *Netochka Nezvanova*. Translated by Ann Dunningan. Englewood Cliffs, NJ: Prentice-Hall, 1970.

———[Fyodor Dostoevsky]. "The Meek One," *Diary of a Writer*. Translated by Boris Brazol. New York: C. Scribner, 1949.

———[Fyodor Dostoyevsky]. *Mr.Prokharchin*. Translated by Constance Garnett.

———[Fyodor Dostoevsky]. *Poor Folk; The Gambler*. Translated by C. J. Hogarth. London: Dent, Everyman Library, 1975.

———[Fyodor Dostoevsky]. *The Raw Youth*. Translated by Constance Garnett. N.p.: Create Space, 2017.

———. *Sobranie sochinenii v 12 tomakh*. Moscow, Russia: Pravda, 1982.

———. *Sobranie sochinenii v 15 tomakh*. Leningrad, Russia: Nauka, 1989–1996.

Fanger, Donald. *Dostoevsky and Romantic Realism: A Study of Dostoevsky in Relation to Balzac, Dickens, and Gogol*. Cambridge, MA: Harvard University Press, 1965.

Frank, Joseph. *Dostoevsky. The Seeds of Revolt. 1821–1849*. Princeton, NJ: Princeton University Press, 1976.

———. *Dostoevsky. The Years of Ordeal. 1850–1859*. Princeton, NJ: Princeton University Press, 1983.

———. *Dostoevsky. The Stir of Liberation. 1860–1865*. Princeton, NJ: Princeton University Press, 1986.

———. *Dostoevsky. The Miraculous Years. 1865–1871.* Princeton, NJ: Princeton University Press, 1995.

———. *Dostoevsky. The Mantle of the Prophet. 1871–1881.* Princeton, NJ: Princeton University Press, 2002.

Gall, Franz Joseph. *Sur l'origine des qualites morales et des facultes intellectuelles.* Vol. 2: *Sur la pluralite des organes cerebraux.* London, UK: Forgotten Books, 2017.

Garcin, Etiènne. *Nouveau dictionnaire provençal-français.* Draguignan, France: Chez Fabre, 1841.

Gareau, Michel, and Beauvais, Lydia. *Charles Le Brun. First Painter to King Louis XIV.* New York: Abrams, 1992.

Giraud, Raymond. *The Unheroic Hero in the Novels of Stendhal, Balzac, and Flaubert.* Whitefish, MT: Literary Licensing, LLC, 2011.

Grossman, Leonid. *Balzac en Russie.* Paris, France: Revue de Press Etrangère, 1946.

———. *Balzac and Dostoevsky.* Translated by Lena Karpov. New York: Ardis, 1973.

———. *Dostoevskii. Put'. Poetika. Tvorchestvo.* Moscow, Russia: Sovremennye problemy, 1928.

———. *Dostoevskii.* Moscow, Russia: Molodaia gvardiia, 1965.

Hall, Jason Y. "Gall's Phrenology: A Romantic Psychology." *Studies in Romanticism.* 16, no. 3: *Romanticism and Science* (Summer 1977): 305–317.

The Holy Bible: King James Version. Chicago: Gideons International, 1961.

Hunt, Joel. "Color Imagery in Dostoevskij and Balzac." *The Slavic and East European Journal* 10, no. 4 (Winter 1966): 411–423.

Illiustrirovannaia Bibleiskaia entsiklopediia Arkhimandrita Nikofora. Moscow, Russia: Eksmo, 2015.

Illiustrirovannyi entsiklopedicheskii slovar'. Edited by V. Borodulin. Moscow, Russia: Autopan, 1998.

James, Henry. "The Lesson of Balzac. Two Lectures." *Atlantic Monthly* (August 1905): 166–180.

Jackson, Robert Louis. *Dostoevsky's Quest for Form: A Study of His Philosophy of Art.* New Haven, CT: Yale University Press, 1966.

Jonge, Alex de. *Dostoevsky and the Age of Intensity.* New York: St. Martin Press, 1975.

Karaulov, Iurii, ed. *Slovar' iazyka Dostoevskogo.* Moscow, Russia: Azbuka, 2008.

Larousse Dictionnaire de l'Histoire de France, 2005.

www.larousse.fr/archives/histoire_de_france/page/879.

Lavater, Johann Caspar. *Essays on Physiognomy.* Translated by Thomas Holcroft. London, UK: Ward, Lock, 1804.

Leatherbarrow, W. J., ed. *The Cambridge Companion to Dostoevsky.* Cambridge, UK: Cambridge University Press, 2002.

Leshnevskaia, Aleksandra. "Tri 'Grande.'" *Inostrannaia literatura* 4(2008). http://magazines.russ.ru/inostran/2008/4/le5.html.

Liddell, Henry George and Robert Scott. *A Greek-English Lexicon.* Revised and Augmented by Sir Henry Stewart Jones. Oxford, UK: Clarendon Press, 1940.

Lotman, Iurii. "Russkaia literatura na frantsuzskom iazyke." In his *Izbrannye stat'i*, vol. 2, 350-369. Tallinn, Estonia: Aleksandra, 1992.

Lynch, Lawrence W. "People, Animals, and Transformations in *Eugénie Grandet*." *The International Fiction Review*, February 09, 2017. https://journals.lib.unb.ca/index.php/IFR/article/view/13620/14703.

Maurois, André. *Prometheus: The Life of Balzac.* London: Penguin, 1971.

Meyer, Priscilla. *How the Russians Read the French.* Madison, WI: Wisconsin University Press, 2008.

Molière, Jean-Baptiste. *The Miser and Other Plays.* London: Penguin Classics, 2000.

Mortimer, Armine Kotin. *For Love or for Money: Balzac's Rhetorical Realism.* Columbus, OH: Ohio State University Press, 2011.

Pushkin, Aleksandr. "Skupoi rytsar'." In his *Polnoe sobranie sochinenii*, vol. 7, 99–121. Moscow, Russia: Voskresenie, 1995.

———[Alexander Pushkin]. *The Covetous Knight*, translated by Irina Zheleznova. http://ocls.kyivlibs.org.ua/pushkin/perekladi_1/Pushkin_english/The_Covetous_Knight/The_Covetous_Knight.htm.

Rice, James L. *Dostoevsky and the Healing Art: An Essay in Literary and Medical History.* Ann Arbor, MI: Ardis, 1985.

Rivers, Christopher. *Face Value: Physiognomical Thought and the Legible Body in Marivaux, Lavater, Balzac, Gautier, and Zola.* Madison, WI: University of Wisconsin Press, 1994.

Rogers, Samuel. *Balzac and the Novel.* New York: Oktagon Books, 1969.

Schacter, Daniel L. *Searching for Memory: The Brain, the Mind, and the Past.* New York: Basic Books, 1996.

Shaikevich, Anatolii. *Statisticheskii slovar' iazyka Dostoevskogo.* Moscow, Russia: Rossiiskaia akademiia nauk, 2003.

Surville, Laure, and Honoré de Balzac. *Balzac, Sa vie et ses oeuvres d'apres sa correspondance.* Paris: Calmann Lèvy, 1858.

———. *The correspondence of Honoré de Balzac. With a Memoir by His Sister, Madame de Surville.* Translated by C. Lamb Kenney. London, UK: R. Bentley, 1878.

Taine, Hyppolite. *Balzac, sa vie son oevres.* Bruxelles: Edition H. Dumond, 1858.

———. *Balzac; a Critical Study.* Translated by Lorenzo O'Rourke. Folcroft, PA: Folcroft Library Editions, 1973.

Terras, Victor. *The Young Dostoevsky (1846–1849): A Critical Study.* The Hague: Mouton, 1969.

Tolkovyi slovar' Ushakova onlain. https://ushakovdictionary.ru/.

Vassmer, Max [Maks Fassmer]. *Etimologicheskii slovar' russkogo iazyka.* Translated by O. N. Trubachev, edited by B. A. Larin. Moscow, Russia: Progress, 1986.

Venuti, Lawrence, ed. *The Translation Studies Reader.* London: Routledge, 2000.

———. *The Translator's Invisibility. A History of Translation*. London and New York. Routledge, 1995.

Vinogradov, Viktor. *O iazyke khudozhestvennoi prozy*. Moscow, Russia: Nauka, 1980.

Wechsler, Judith. *A Human Comedy: Physiognomy and Caricature in 19th-Century Paris*. Chicago: University of Chicago Press, 1982.

Woodsworth, Judith. *Telling the Story of Translation: Writers who Translate*. London, New York: Bloomsbury Academic, 2017.

Zweig, Stefan. *Balzac, Dickens, Dostoevsky: Master Builders of the Spirit*. Somerset, NJ: Transaction, 2010.

———. *Balzac*. Translated by William Rose, Dorothy Rose, and Richard Friedenthal. New York: Viking, 1946.

Index

CPSIA information can be obtained
at www.ICGtesting.com
Printed in the USA
BVHW050809200323
660346BV00013B/9